Gift from
Stella Slazik
219 Henry St
Rome NY
1979

USA—THE MESSAGE
OF JUSTICE, PEACE AND LOVE

U.S.A.

THE MESSAGE OF JUSTICE, PEACE AND LOVE

JOHN PAUL II

Compiled and Indexed
by the Daughters of St. Paul

ST. PAUL EDITIONS

Reprinted with permission from *L'Osservatore Romano,* English Edition.

Library of Congress Cataloging in Publication Data

John Paul II, Pope, 1920- .
    U.S.A.—the message of justice, peace and love.

    Reprinted from L'Osservatore romano, English weekly edition.

    1. Theology, Catholic—Addresses, essays, lectures.
2. United States—Religion—1945-   —Addresses,
essays, lectures. I. Daughters of St. Paul.
II. Title.
BX1755.J65   230'.2   79-24936

Printed in U.S.A. by the Daughters of St. Paul
50 St. Paul's Ave., Boston, Ma. 02130

The Daughters of St. Paul are an international congregation of religious women serving the Church with the communications media.

CONTENTS

FOREWORD

At the usual meeting with the faithful for the recitation of the Angelus on Sunday, September 23, the Holy Father delivered the following address.

...Saturday, September 29, I will go on a journey to Ireland, from whence I will continue to the United States of America on October 1. As I have already mentioned previously, the first incentive for this journey was the invitation of the Secretary-General of the U.N.O., Dr. Kurt Waldheim. It was addressed to me by this illustrious statesman shortly after the beginning of the Pontificate, and was then renewed at the meeting in May of this year. I attach great importance to the task that my presence before the Assembly of the United Nations imposes on me, and today, once more, I ask everyone for the spiritual aid of prayer.

...It is a good thing that our way to New York, to the session of U.N.O., should pass through Ireland, so as to become, in this way, a new pilgrimage along the paths of papal service of the Church. It is a good thing that this pilgrimage should be continued in the United States, as a visit to that Church and that society. I am grateful for the invitation of the Episcopal Conference of the USA, as well as for the invitation that Mr. Jimmy Carter, President of the United States of America, addressed to me at the same time. Planning to stay in

America till Sunday, October 7 (I cannot stay any longer, since my duties call me to Rome), I am not able to respond to all the individual invitations which have reached the Secretariat of State in large numbers, in the last few weeks. Today, on the other hand, I wish to express my heartfelt thanks for these invitations and for the many proofs of goodwill.

Travelling along the ways chosen by the pilgrimage, I will try to meet the appeal which, from so many communities and so many hearts, reaches the unworthy Successor of St. Peter in Rome. I ask them all for a prayer, in order that I may carry out this service of mine in the land of Washington, for the glory of God and for the good of men, my beloved brothers and sisters.

AMERICA, "GOD SHED HIS GRACE ON THEE"

Awaiting the Pope at Logan Airport in Boston on October 1, 1979, were numerous Cardinals, Mrs. Jimmy Carter, wife of President Carter, high officials of the State of Massachusetts and the city of Boston, as well as a large gathering of people.

After listening to an address of welcome by Mrs. Carter the Holy Father spoke as follows:

Praised be Jesus Christ!

It is a great joy for me to be in the United States of America, to begin my pastoral visit to the Catholic Church in this land, and at the same time to greet all the American people, of every race, color and creed.

I am grateful for the cordial welcome given me on behalf of President Carter, whom I thank most sincerely for his invitation to the United States. I am looking forward to meeting the president after my visit to the United Nations.

My thanks go also to the Cardinal Archbishop of Boston, who in this historic city offers me the first hospitality of this country. I am grateful to the episcopal conference and to all the individual bishops who have so kindly asked me to come. My only regret is that I cannot accept all the invitations extended to me by religious and civil officials, by individuals, families and groups.

From so many quarters—Catholics, Protestants and Jews—America has opened her heart to me. And on my part I come to you—America—with sentiments of friendship, reverence and esteem. I come as one who already knows you and loves you, as one who

17

wishes you to fulfill completely your noble destiny of service to the world. Once again I can now admire firsthand the beauty of this vast land stretching between two oceans; once again I am experiencing the warm hospitality of the American people.

Although it is not possible for me to enter into every home, to greet personally every man and woman, to caress every child in whose eyes is reflected the innocence of love—still, I feel close to all of you, and you are all in my prayers.

Permit me to express my sentiments in the lyrics of your own song: "America! America! God shed His grace on thee, and crown thy good with brotherhood, from sea to shining sea."

And may the peace of the Lord be with you always—America!

"I AM HAPPY
TO BE IN YOUR MIDST"

A crowd estimated at two million lined the route along which passed the cortege of cars that accompanied the Holy Father from the airport into the city of Boston on October 1. Stopping at the Cathedral of Holy Cross, the Holy Father met the diocesan and religious clergy, and the religious women of the Archdiocese of Boston and other dioceses of New England. The assembly of more than two thousand persons was led by Cardinal Humberto Medeiros, who delivered an address of welcome. After a brief Liturgy of the Word, Pope John Paul spoke to the group as follows:

Dear Cardinal Medeiros, dear brothers and sisters in Christ,

On the first day of my pastoral visit to the United States of America, it is a great joy for me to come to this City of Boston, and in this Cathedral, and later tonight on the Common, to be able to meet with the Catholic community. It is the first time in history that a Successor of Peter is received in your midst. On this wonderful occasion I wish to render homage to the Most Holy Trinity, in whose name I have come. And I make my own the greeting of the Apostle Paul to the Corinthians: "To you who have been consecrated in Christ Jesus and called to be a holy people, and to all those who, wherever they may be, call on the name of our Lord Jesus Christ, their Lord and ours: Grace and peace from God our Father and the Lord Jesus Christ'' (1 Cor. 1:2-3).

My cordial thanks go to you, Cardinal Medeiros, Archbishop of Boston, for your welcome today. In your Cathedral Church, I am happy to renew to you the expression of my deep esteem and friendship. Warm greetings also to the Auxiliary Bishops and to all the clergy, both diocesan and religious: you who are my brother priests in virtue of the Sacrament of Holy Orders. Through your priesthood, you are also God's gift to the Christian community. Because you are servants of the Gospel, you will always be close to the people and their problems. Because you share in the Priesthood of Christ, your presence in the world shall always be marked by Christ's zeal, for He set you apart so that you might build up His Body, the Church (cf. Eph. 4:12).

I wish to extend a special blessing to you religious, both religious brothers and sisters, who have consecrated your lives to Jesus Christ. May you always find joy in His love. And to all of you, the laity of this Diocese, who are united with the Cardinal and the clergy in a common mission, I open my heart in love and trust. You are the workers for evangelization in the realities of daily life, and you give witness to the love of Christ in the service that you give to all your fellow men and women, beginning with your own families.

To all I want to say how happy I am to be in your midst. I pray for each one of you, asking you to remain always united in Jesus Christ and His Church, so that together we may ''display to the world our unity in proclaiming the mystery of Christ, in revealing the divine dimension and also the human perseverance for the dignity that each human being has reached and can continually reach in Christ" *(Redemptor hominis,* 11). May this Cathedral, dedicated to the Holy Cross of Jesus, always be a reminder of our calling to greatness, for through the mystery of the Incarnation and of the redeeming sacrifice of Jesus on the cross we share in "the unsearchable riches of Christ" (Eph. 3:8).

From this Cathedral I send my greeting to all the people of this city of Boston: to those in particular who are, in one way or another, burdened by suffering; to the sick and the bedridden; to those whom society seems to have left by the wayside, and those who have lost faith in God and in their fellow human beings. To all, I have come with a message of hope and peace—the hope and peace of Jesus Christ, for whom every human being is of immense value and dignity, and in whom are found all the treasures of justice and love.

In the city of Boston I am greeting a community that through the many upheavals of history has always been able to change and yet to remain true to itself—a community where people of all backgrounds, creeds, races and convictions have provided workable solutions to problems and have created a home where all people can be respected in their human dignity. For the honor of all the citizens of Boston, who have inherited a tradition of fraternal love and concern, may I recall what one of the founders of this city told his fellow-settlers as they were aboard ship en route to their new home in America: "We must love one another with a pure heart fervently, we must bear one another's burdens." These simple words explain so much of the meaning of life—our life as brothers and sisters in our Lord Jesus Christ.

May God's peace descend on this city of Boston and bring joy to every conscience and joy to every heart!

I REPEAT
WITH CHRIST:
"COME, FOLLOW ME!"

The great Boston Common was the scene of the Holy Father's first concelebrated Mass in the United States on October 1. In the presence of half a million people, the Pope concelebrated Mass with some sixty Bishops from New England and Canada, besides Cardinal Medeiros, Archbishop of Boston, and Cardinal Casaroli, Secretary of State.

During the Mass the Pope preached the following homily.

Dear brothers and sisters, dear young people of America,

1. Earlier today, I set foot on the soil of the United States of America. In the name of Christ I begin a pastoral journey that will take me to several of your cities. At the beginning of this year, I had the occasion to greet this continent and its people from a place where Christopher Columbus landed; today I stand at this gateway to the United States, and again I greet all of America. For its people, wherever they are, have a special place in the love of the Pope.

I come to the United States of America as Successor of Peter and as a pilgrim of faith. It gives me great joy to be able to make this visit. And so, my esteem and affection go out to all the people of this land. I greet all Americans without distinction; I want to meet you and tell you all—men and women of all creeds and ethnic origins, children and youth, fathers and mothers, the sick and the elderly—that God loves you, that He has given you a dignity as human beings

24

that is beyond compare. I want to tell everyone that the Pope is your friend and a servant of your humanity. On this first day of my visit, I wish to express my esteem and love for America itself, for the experience that began two centuries ago and that carries the name "United States of America"; for the past achievements of this land and for its dedication to a more just and human future; for the generosity with which this country has offered shelter, freedom and a chance for betterment to all who have come to its shores; and for the human solidarity that impels you to collaborate with all other nations so that freedom may be safeguarded and full human advancement made possible. I greet you, America the beautiful!

2. I am here because I wanted to respond to the invitation which the Secretary-General of the United Nations Organization first addressed to me. Tomorrow I shall have the honor, as guest of the United Nations, to go to this supreme international forum of nations, and to deliver an address to the General Assembly: to make a plea to the whole world for justice and peace—a plea in defense of the unique dignity of every human being. I feel highly honored by the invitation of the United Nations Secretary-General. At the same time I am conscious of the greatness and importance of the challenge that this invitation brings with it. I have been convinced from the very first that this invitation by the United Nations should be accepted by me *as Bishop of Rome* and *pastor of the Universal Church* of Christ. And so, I express my deep gratitude also to the Hierarchy of the Church in the United States, who joined in the initiative of the United Nations. I have received many invitations from individual dioceses, and from dif-

ferent regions of this country, as well as from Canada. I deeply regret that I am unable to accept all the invitations; I would willingly make a pastoral visit everywhere, if it were possible. My pilgrimage to Ireland on the occasion of the centenary of the Shrine of our Lady at Knock constituted a fitting introduction to my visit with you. I sincerely hope that my whole visit in the United States will be seen in the light of the Second Vatican Council's Constitution on the Church in the Modern World.

And tonight I am deeply pleased to be with you on Boston Common. In you I greet the City of Boston and all its people, as well as the Commonwealth of Massachusetts and all its civil authorities. With special warmth, I greet here Cardinal Medeiros and the whole Archdiocese of Boston. A special remembrance links me with the City, for three years ago, at the invitation of its Divinity School, I had the opportunity to speak at the University of Harvard. As I recall this memorable event, I wish to express once again my gratitude to the authorities of Harvard and to the Dean of the Divinity School for that exceptionally valuable opportunity.

3. During my first visit in the United States as Pope, on the eve of my visit to the United Nations Organization, I now wish to speak a special word to the young people that are gathered here.

Tonight, in a very special way, I hold out my hands to the youth of America. In Mexico City and Guadalajara I met the youth of Latin America. In Warsaw and Krakow I met the youth of Poland. In Rome I meet frequently groups of young people from Italy and from all over the world. Yesterday I met the youth of Ireland in Galway. And now with great joy I meet you. For me, each one of these meetings is a new discovery. Again and again I find in young people the joy and enthusiasm of life, a searching for truth and for the deeper meaning of the existence that unfolds before them in all its attraction and potential.

4. Tonight, I want to repeat what I keep telling youth: you are the future of the world, and "the day of tomorrow belongs to you." I want to remind you of the encounters that Jesus Himself had with the youth of His day. The Gospels preserve for us a striking account of a conversation Jesus had with a young man. We read there that the young man put to Christ one of the fundamental questions that youth everywhere ask: "What must I do...?" (Mk. 10:17), and he received a precise and penetrating answer. "Then, Jesus looked at him with love and told him...'Come and follow me' " (Mk. 10:21). But see what happens: the young man, who had shown such interest in the fundamental question, "went away sad, for he had many possessions" (Mk. 10:22). Yes, he went away, and—as can be deduced from the context —he refused to accept the call of Christ.

This deeply penetrating event, in its concise eloquence, expresses a great lesson in a few words: it touches upon substantial problems and basic questions that have in no way lost their relevance. Everywhere young people are asking important questions—questions on the meaning of life, on the right way to live, on the true scale of values: "What must I do...?" "What must I do to share in everlasting life?" This questioning bears witness to your thoughts, your consciences, your hearts and wills. This questioning tells the world that you, young people, carry within yourselves a special openness with regard to what is good and what is true. This openness is, in a sense, a "revelation" of the human spirit. And in this openness to truth, to goodness and to beauty, each one of you can find yourself; indeed, in this openness you can all experience in some measure what the young man in the Gospel experienced: "Jesus looked at him with love" (Mk. 10:21).

5. To each one of you I say therefore: heed the call of Christ when you hear Him saying to you: "Follow me!" Walk in my path! Stand by my side! Remain in my love! There is a choice to be made: a choice for Christ and His way of life, and His commandment of love.

The message of love that Christ brought is always important, always relevant. It is not difficult to see how today's world, despite its beauty and grandeur, despite the conquests of science and technology, despite the refined and abundant material goods that it offers, is yearning for more truth, for more love, for more joy. And all of this is found in Christ and in His way of life.

Do I then make a mistake when I tell you, Catholic youth, that it is part of your task in the world and the Church to reveal the true meaning of life where hatred, neglect or selfishness threaten to take over the world? Faced with problems and disappointments, many people will try to escape from their responsibility: escape in selfishness, escape in sexual pleasure, escape in drugs, escape in violence, escape in indifference and cynical attitudes. But today, I propose to you the option of love, which is the opposite of escape. If you really accept that love from Christ, it will lead you to God. Perhaps in the priesthood or religious life; perhaps in some special service to your

brothers and sisters: especially to the needy, the poor, the lonely, the abandoned, those whose rights have been trampled upon, or those whose basic needs have not been provided for. Whatever you make of your life, let it be something that reflects the love of Christ. The whole People of God will be all the richer because of the diversity of your commitments. In whatever you do, remember that Christ is calling you, in one way or another, to the service of love: the love of God and of your neighbor.

6. And now coming back to the story of the young man in the Gospels, we see that he heard the call— "Follow me"—but that he "went away sad, for he had many possessions."

The sadness of the young man makes us reflect. We could be tempted to think that many possessions, many of the goods of this world, can bring happiness. We see instead in the case of the young man in the Gospel that his many possessions had become an obstacle to accepting the call of Jesus to follow Him. He was not ready to say *yes* to Jesus, and *no* to self, to say *yes* to love and *no* to escape.

Real love is demanding. I would fail in my mission if I did not clearly tell you so. For it was Jesus—our Jesus Himself—who said: "You are my friends if you do what I command you" (Jn. 15:14). Love demands effort and a personal commitment to the will of God. It means discipline and sacrifice, but it also means joy and human fulfillment.

Dear young people: do not be afraid of honest effort and honest work; do not be afraid of the truth. With Christ's help, and through prayer, you can answer His call, resisting temptations and fads, and every form of mass manipulation. Open your hearts to the Christ of the Gospels—to His love and His truth and His joy. Do not go away sad!

And, as a last word to all of you who listen to me tonight, I would say this: the reason for my mission, for my journey, through the United States is to tell you, to tell everyone—young and old alike—to say to everyone in the name of Christ: "Come and follow me!"

Follow Christ! You who are married: share your love and your burdens with each other; respect the human dignity of your spouse; accept joyfully the life that God gives through you; make your marriage stable and secure for your children's sake.

Follow Christ! You who are single or who are preparing for marriage. Follow Christ! You who are young or old. Follow Christ! You who are sick or aging; who are suffering or in pain. You who feel the need for healing, the need for love, the need for a friend—follow Christ!

To all of you I extend—in the name of Christ—the call, the invitation, the plea: "Come and follow me." This is why I have come to America, and why I have come to Boston tonight: to call you to Christ—to call all of you and each of you to live in His love, today and forever. Amen!

"THERE IS ONLY
ONE WORLD..."

On October 2, the Holy Father was met at La Guardia Airport in New York by Kurt Waldheim, Secretary-General of the United Nations, who gave an address of welcome. Present also were the highest Authorities of the city and state. In response to Mr. Waldheim's address of welcome, the Pope spoke as follows.

Mr. Secretary-General,
Ladies and gentlemen,

I reply with deep gratitude to the greetings of the Secretary-General of the United Nations Organization. I have looked forward to this moment since the day he extended to me, immediately after the beginning of my pontificate, the invitation to address the Thirty-fourth General Assembly. Your kind initiative, that honors me greatly, was thus at the basis of the journey that has taken me first to Ireland and that I shall continue in the United States of America.

Your Organization has a special significance for the whole world, for in it the needs and the aspirations of all the people of our planet come together. The supreme international forum that it is brings together the efforts and the determination of all men and women of good will, who have resolved to honor the pledge that the founders of the United Nations made thirty-four years ago and inscribed in the first article of the Charter: to work together to harmonize the actions of the nations in the attainment of international peace and security, to develop friendly relations among nations, to achieve international cooperation, and to promote respect for human rights and for fundamental freedoms for all without distinction as to race, sex, language or religion.

The very first day after the solemn beginning of my ministry as Supreme Pastor of the Catholic Church, in addressing the representatives of the States and the International Organizations, I took the opportunity to express my esteem for the important role of the International Organizations, and of the United Nations in particular. Here I wish to state again how greatly I value your Institution. For as I stated on that other occasion: "You are the first to be convinced that there can be no true human progress or lasting peace without the courageous, loyal and disinterested pursuit of growing cooperation and unity among people" (October 23, 1978).

Yes, the conviction that unites us in this common service of humanity is that, at the basis of all efforts, there must be "the dignity and worth of the human person" (Charter, Preamble). It is likewise the human person—every individual—who must make the aims of your Organization come true in the concrete realities of friendly relations, of tolerance, of freedom and harmony for all. Decisions and resolutions can be adopted by the representatives of the nations, but their true embodiment will have to be brought about by the people.

Through you then, Mr. Secretary-General and distinguished ladies and gentlemen, at the beginning of my visit to the United Nations, I greet all the men, women and children of the countries that are represented at the United Nations. May the hopes that they place in the efforts and in the solidarity that link us all never be disappointed. May they experience in the achievements of the United Nations the fact that there is only one world, and that it is the home of all.

Thank you, and may God sustain you in your high ideals.

ADDRESS TO THE XXXIV GENERAL ASSEMBLY OF THE UNITED NATIONS ORGANIZATION

At the General Assembly of the United Nations on Tuesday, October 2, His Holiness John Paul II delivered his appeal for peace and human rights to the representatives of 151 countries and through them to all inhabitants of the earth.

It was the Pope's second day in the United States of America.

After addresses of welcome by Mr. Salim Ahmed Salim and Dr. Kurt Waldheim, President of the General Assembly and Secretary-General respectively of the United Nations Organization, Pope John Paul delivered the following address.

Mr. President,

1. I desire to express my gratitude to the General Assembly of the United Nations, which I am permitted today to participate in and to address. My thanks go in the first place to the Secretary-General of the United Nations Organization, Dr. Kurt Waldheim. Last autumn, soon after my election to the Chair of St. Peter, he invited me to make this visit, and he renewed his invitation in the course of our meeting in Rome last May. From the first moment I felt greatly honored and deeply obliged. And today, before this distinguished Assembly, I also thank you, Mr. President, who have so kindly welcomed me and invited me to speak.

2. *The formal reason for my intervention* today is, without any question, the special bond of cooperation that links the Apostolic See with the United Nations Organization, as is shown by the presence of the Holy See's Permanent Observer to this Organization. The existence of this bond, which is held in high esteem by the Holy See, rests on the sovereignty with which the Apostolic See has been endowed for many centuries. The territorial extent of that sovereignty is limited to the small State of Vatican City, but the sovereignty itself is warranted by the need of the papacy to exercise its mission in full freedom, and to be able to deal with any interlocutor, whether a government or an international organization, without dependence on other sovereignties. Of course the nature and aims of the spiritual mission of the Apostolic See and the Church make their participation in the tasks and activities of the United Nations Organization very different from that of the States, which are communities in the political and temporal sense.

3. Besides attaching great importance to its collaboration with the United Nations Organization, *the Apostolic See has always, since the foundation of your Organization, expressed its esteem and its agreement* with the historic significance of this supreme forum for the international life of humanity today. It also never ceases to support your Organization's function and initiatives, which are aimed at peaceful coexistence and collaboration between nations. There are many proofs of this. In the more than thirty years of the existence of the United Nations Organization, it has received much attention in papal messages and encyclicals, in documents of the Catholic episcopate,

and likewise in the Second Vatican Council. Pope John XXIII and Pope Paul VI looked with confidence on your important institution as an eloquent and promising sign of our times. He who is now addressing you has, since the first months of his pontificate, several times expressed the same confidence and conviction as his predecessors.

4. This confidence and conviction on the part of the Apostolic See is the result, as I have said, not of merely political reasons but of the religious and moral character of *the mission of the Roman Catholic Church.* As a universal community embracing faithful belonging to almost all countries and continents, nations, peoples, races, languages and cultures, the Church is deeply interested in the existence and activity of *the Organization* whose very name tells us that it *unites and associates* nations and States. It unites and associates: it does not divide and oppose. It seeks out the ways for understanding and peaceful collaboration, and endeavors with the means at its disposal and the methods in its power to exclude war, division and mutual destruction within the great family of humanity today.

5. This is the real reason, *the essential reason,* for my presence among you, and I wish to thank this distinguished Assembly for giving consideration to this reason, which can make my presence among you in some way useful. It is certainly a highly significant fact that among the representatives of the States, whose *raison d'être* is the sovereignty of powers linked with territory and people, there is also today the representative of the Apostolic See and the Catholic Church. This Church is the Church of Jesus Christ, who declared before the tribunal of the

Roman judge Pilate that He was a King, but with a
kingdom not of this world (cf. Jn. 18:36-37). When He
was then asked about the reason for the existence of
His kingdom among men, He explained: "For this I
was born, and for this I have come into the world, to
bear witness to the truth" (Jn 18:37). Here, *before the
representatives of the States,* I wish not only to thank
you but also to offer my special *congratulations,* since
the invitation extended to the Pope to speak in your
Assembly shows that *the United Nations Organization
accepts and respects* the religious and moral dimension
of those human problems that the Church attends to,
in view of the message of truth and love that it is her
duty to bring to the world. The questions that concern
your functions and receive your attention—as is indicated by the vast organic complex of institutions
and activities that are part of or collaborate with the
United Nations, especially in the fields of culture,
health, food, labor, and the peaceful uses of nuclear
energy—certainly make it essential for us *to meet in
the name of man in his wholeness,* in all the fullness and
manifold riches of his spiritual and material existence, as I have stated in my encyclical *Redemptor
hominis,* the first of my pontificate.

6. Now, availing myself of the solemn occasion of
my meeting with the representatives of the nations of
the earth, I wish above all to send my greetings to all
the men and women living on this planet. To every
man and every woman, without any exception whatever. Every human being living on earth is a member
of a civil society, of a nation, many of them represented here. Each one of you, distinguished ladies and
gentlemen, represents a particular State, system and
political structure, but what you represent above

all are *individual human beings;* you are all *representa-tives of men and women, of practically all the people of the world,* individual men and women, communities and peoples who are living the present phase of their own history and who are also part of the history of humanity as a whole, each of them a subject endowed with dignity as a human person, with his or her own culture, experiences and aspirations, tensions and sufferings, and legitimate expectations. This relationship is what provides the reason for *all political activity,* whether national or international, for in the final analysis this activity comes *from man,* is exercised *by man* and is *for man.* And if political activity is cut off from this fundamental relationship and finality, if it becomes in a way its own end, it loses much of its reason to exist. Even more, it can also give rise to a specific alienation; it can become extraneous to man; it can come to contradict humanity itself. In reality, what justifies the existence of any political activity is service to man, concerned and responsible attention to the essential problems and duties of his earthly existence in its social dimension and significance, on which also the good of each person depends.

7. I ask you, ladies and gentlemen, to excuse me for speaking of questions that are certainly self-evident for you. But it does not seem pointless to speak of them, since the most frequent pitfall for human activities is the possibility of losing sight, while performing them, of *the clearest truths, the most elementary principles.*

I would like to express the wish that, in view of its universal character, the United Nations Organization will never cease to be the forum, *the high tribune from which all man's problems are appraised in truth and justice.* It was in the name of this inspiration, it was through this historic stimulus, that on June 26, 1945, towards the end of the terrible Second World War, the Charter of the United Nations was signed and on the following October 24 your Organization began its life. Soon after, on December 10, 1948, came its fundamental. document, the *Universal Declaration of Human Rights,* the rights of the human being as a concrete individual and of the human being in his universal value. This document is a milestone on the long and difficult path of the human race. The progress of humanity must be measured not only by *the progress of science and technology,* which shows man's uniqueness with regard to nature, but also and chiefly by *the primacy given to spiritual values* and by *the progress of moral life.* In this field is manifested the full dominion of reason, through truth, in the behavior of the individual and of society, and also the control of reason over nature; and thus human conscience quietly triumphs, as was expressed in the ancient saying: *"Genus humanum arte et ratione vivit."*

It was when technology was being directed in its one-sided progress towards goals of war, hegemony and conquest, so that man might kill man and nation destroy nation by depriving it of its liberty and the right to exist—and I still have before my mind the image of the Second World War in Europe, which began forty years ago on September 1, 1939, with the invasion of Poland and ended on May 9, 1945—it was precisely then that the United Nations Organization arose. And three years later the document appeared which, as I have said, must be considered a real milestone on the path of the moral progress of humanity—the *Universal Declaration of Human Rights.* The governments and States of the world have understood that, if they are not to attack and destroy each other, *they must unite.* The real way, the fundamental *way to this is through each human being,* through the definition and recognition of and respect for the inalienable rights of individuals and of the communities of peoples.

8. Today, forty years after the outbreak of the Second World War, I wish to recall the whole of the experiences by individuals and nations that were sustained by a generation that is largely still alive. I had occasion not long ago to reflect again on some of those experiences, in one of the places that are most distressing and overflowing with contempt for man and his fundamental rights—the extermination camp of Oswiecim (Auschwitz), which I visited during my pilgrimage to Poland last June. This infamous place is unfortunately only one of the many scattered over the continent of Europe. But the memory of even one should be *a warning sign* on the path of humanity today, in order that *every kind of concentration camp* anywhere on earth may once and for all *be done away with.* And everything that recalls those horrible experiences should also disappear forever from the lives of nations and States, everything that is a continuation of those experiences under different forms, namely, the various kinds of torture and oppression, either physical or moral, carried out under any system, in any land; this phenomenon is all the more distressing if it occurs under the pretext of internal ''security'' or the need to preserve an apparent peace.

9. You will forgive me, ladies and gentlemen, for evoking this memory. But I would be untrue to the

history of this century, I would be dishonest with regard to the great cause of man, which we all wish to serve, if I should keep silent, I who come from the country on whose living body Oswiecim was at one time constructed. But my purpose in evoking this memory is above all to show what painful experiences and sufferings by millions of people gave rise to the Universal Declaration of Human Rights, which has been placed as the basic inspiration and *cornerstone* of the United Nations Organization. This Declaration was paid for by millions of our brothers and sisters at the cost of their suffering and sacrifice, brought about by the brutalization that darkened and made insensitive the human consciences of their oppressors and of those who carried out a real genocide. This price cannot have been paid in vain! The Universal Declaration of Human Rights—with its train of many declarations and conventions on highly important aspects of human rights, in favor of children, of women, of equality between races, and especially the two international covenants on economic, social and cultural rights and on civil and political rights—must remain the basic value in the United Nations Organization with which the consciences of its members must be confronted and from which they must draw continual inspiration. If the truths and principles contained in this document were to be forgotten or ignored and were thus to lose the genuine self-evidence that distinguished them at the time they were brought painfully to birth, then the noble purpose of the United Nations Organization could be faced with the threat of a new destruction. This is what would happen if the simple yet powerful eloquence of the Universal Declaration of Human Rights were de-

cisively subjugated by what is wrongly called political interest, but often really means no more than one-sided gain and advantage to the detriment of others, or a thirst for power regardless of the needs of others—everything which by its nature is opposed to the spirit of the Declaration. "Political interest" understood in this sense, if you will pardon me, ladies and gentlemen, dishonors the noble and difficult mission of your service for the good of your countries and of all humanity.

10. Fourteen years ago my great predecessor *Pope Paul VI* spoke from this podium. He spoke memorable words, which I desire to repeat today: "No more war, war never again! Never one against the other," or even "one above the other," but always, on every occasion, "with each other."

Paul VI was a tireless servant of the cause of peace. I wish to follow him with all my strength and continue his service. The Catholic Church in every place on earth proclaims a message of peace, prays for peace, *educates for peace.* This purpose is also shared by the representatives and followers of other Churches and Communities and of other religions of the world, and they have pledged themselves to it. In union with efforts by all people of good will, this work is certainly bearing fruit. Nevertheless we are continually troubled by the armed conflicts that break out from time to time. How grateful we are to the Lord when a direct intervention succeeds in avoiding such a conflict, as in the case of the tension that last year threatened Argentina and Chile.

It is my fervent hope that a solution also to the Middle East crises may draw nearer. While being prepared to recognize the value of any concrete step or attempt made to settle the conflict, I want to recall that it would have no value if it did not truly represent the "first stone" of a general overall peace in the area, a peace that, being necessarily based on equitable recognition of the rights of all, cannot fail to include the consideration and just settlement of the Palestinian question. Connected with this question is that of the tranquillity, independence and territorial integrity of Lebanon within the formula that has made it an example of peaceful and mutually fruitful coexistence between distinct communities, a formula that I hope will, in the common interest, be maintained, with the adjustments required by the developments of the situation. I also hope for a special statute that, under international guarantees—as my predecessor Paul VI indicated—would respect the particular nature of Jerusalem, a heritage sacred to the veneration of millions of believers of the three great monotheistic religions, Judaism, Christianity and Islam.

We are troubled also by reports of the development of weaponry exceeding in quality and size the means of war and destruction ever known before. In this field also we applaud the decisions and agreements aimed at reducing the arms race. Nevertheless, the life of humanity today is seriously endangered by the threat of destruction and by the risk arising even from accepting certain "tranquillizing" reports. And the resistance to actual concrete proposals of real disarmament, such as those called for by this assembly in a special session last year, shows that together with the will for peace that all profess and that most desire there is also in existence—perhaps in latent or conditional form but nonetheless real—the contrary and the negation of this will. The continual *preparations for war* demonstrated by the production of ever more numerous, powerful and sophisticated weapons in various countries show that there is a desire to be ready for war, and *being ready* means *being able to start it;* it also means taking the risk that sometime, somewhere, somehow, someone can set in motion the terrible mechanism of general destruction.

11. It is therefore necessary to make a continuing and even more energetic effort to do away with the very possibility of provoking war, and to make such catastrophes impossible by influencing the attitudes and convictions, the very intentions and aspirations of governments and peoples. This duty, kept constantly in mind by the United Nations Organization and each of its institutions, must also be a duty for every society, every regime, every government. This task is certainly served by initiatives aimed at international cooperation for the fostering of development. As Paul VI said at the end of his encyclical *Populorum progressio,* "If the new name for peace is development, who would not wish to labor for it with all his powers?" However, this task must also be served by constant reflection and activity aimed at *discovering the very roots* of hatred, destructiveness and contempt—the roots of everything that produces the temptation to war, not so much in the hearts of the nations as in the inner determination of the systems that decide the history of whole societies. In this titanic labor of building up the peaceful future of our planet the United Nations Organization has undoubtedly a key function and guiding role, for which it must refer to the just ideals contained in the Universal Declara-

tion of Human Rights. For this Declaration has struck a real blow against the many deep roots of war, since the spirit of war, in its basic primordial meaning, springs up and grows to maturity where the inalienable rights of man are violated.

This is a new and deeply relevant vision of the cause of peace, one that goes deeper and is more radical. It is a vision that sees the genesis, and in a sense the substance, of war in the more complex forms emanating from injustice viewed in all its various aspects: this injustice first attacks human rights and thereby destroys the organic unity of the social order and it then affects the whole system of international relations. Within the Church's doctrine, the encyclical *Pacem in terris* by John XXIII provides in synthetic form a view of this matter that is very close to the ideological foundation of the United Nations Organization. This must therefore form the basis to which one must loyally and perseveringly adhere in order to establish true "peace on earth."

12. By applying this criterion we must diligently examine *which principal tensions* in connection with the inalienable rights of man can weaken the construction of this peace which we all desire so ardently and which is the essential goal of the efforts of the United Nations Organization. It is not easy, but it must be done. Anyone who undertakes it must take up a totally objective position and be guided by sincerity, readiness to acknowledge one's prejudices and mistakes and readiness even to renounce one's own particular interests, including political interests. Peace is something greater and more important than any of these interests. It is by sacrificing these in-

terests for the sake of peace that we serve them best. After all, in whose "political interest" can it ever be to have another war?

Every analysis must necessarily start from the premise that—although each person lives in a particular concrete social and historical context—every human being is endowed with a dignity that must never be lessened, impaired or destroyed but must instead be respected and safeguarded, if peace is really to be built up.

13. In a movement that one hopes will be progressive and continuous, the Universal Declaration of Human Rights and the other international and national juridical instruments are endeavoring to create general awareness of the dignity of the human being, and to define at least some of the inalienable rights of man. Permit me to enumerate some of the most important human rights that are universally recognized: the right to life, liberty and security of person; the right to food, clothing, housing, sufficient health care, rest and leisure; the right to freedom of expression, education and culture; the right to freedom of thought, conscience and religion, and the right to manifest one's religion either individually or in community, in public or in private; the right to choose a state of life, to found a family and to enjoy all conditions necessary for family life; the right to property and work, to adequate working conditions and a just wage; the right of assembly and association; the right to freedom of movement, to internal and external migration; the right to nationality and residence; the right to political participation and the right to participate in the free choice of the political system of the people to which one belongs. All these human rights

taken together are in keeping with the substance of the dignity of the human being, understood in his entirety, not as reduced to one dimension only. These rights concern the satisfaction of man's essential needs, the exercise of his freedoms, and his relationships with others; but always and everywhere they concern man, they concern man's full human dimension.

14. Man lives at the same time both in the world of material values and in that of spiritual values. For the individual living and hoping man, his needs, freedoms and relationships with others never concern one sphere of values alone, but belong to both. Material and spiritual realities may be viewed separately in order to understand better that in the concrete human being they are inseparable, and to see that any threat to human rights, whether in the field of material realities or in that of spiritual realities, is equally dangerous for peace, since in every instance it concerns man in his entirety. Permit me, distinguished ladies and gentlemen, to recall a constant rule of the history of humanity, a rule that is implicitly contained in all that I have already stated with regard to integral development and human rights. The rule is based on the relationship between spiritual values and material or economic values. In this relationship, it is the spiritual values that are preeminent, both on account of the nature of these values and also for reasons concerning the good of man. The preeminence of the values of the spirit defines the proper sense of earthly material goods and the way to use them. This preeminence is therefore at the basis of a just peace. It is also a contributing factor to ensuring that material development, technical de-

velopment and the development of civilization are at the service of what constitutes man. This means enabling man to have full access to truth, to moral development, and to the complete possibility of enjoying the goods of culture which he has inherited, and of increasing them by his own creativity. It is easy to see that material goods do not have unlimited capacity for satisfying the needs of man: they are not in themselves easily distributed and, in the relationship between those who possess and enjoy them and those who are without them, they give rise to tension, dissension and division that will often even turn into open conflict. Spiritual goods, on the other hand, are open to unlimited enjoyment by many at the same time, without diminution of the goods themselves. Indeed, the more people share in such goods, the more they are enjoyed and drawn upon, the more then do those goods show their indestructible and immortal worth. This truth is confirmed, for example, by the works of creativity—I mean by the works of thought, poetry, music, and the figurative arts, fruits of man's spirit.

15. A critical analysis of our modern civilization shows that in the last hundred years it has contributed as never before to the development of material goods, but that it has also given rise, both in theory and still more in practice, to a series of attitudes in which *sensitivity to the spiritual dimension of human existence is diminished* to a greater or less extent, as a result of certain premises which reduce the meaning of human life chiefly to the many different material and economic factors—I mean to the demands of production, the market, consumption, the accumulation of riches or of the growing bureaucracy

with which an attempt is made to regulate these very processes. Is this not the result of having subordinated man to one single conception and sphere of values?

16. What is the link between these reflections and the cause of peace and war? Since, as I have already stated, material goods by their very nature provoke conditionings and divisions, the struggle to obtain these goods becomes *inevitable in the history of humanity.* If we cultivate this one-sided subordination of man to material goods alone, we shall be incapable of *overcoming this state of need.* We shall be able to attenuate it and avoid it in particular cases, but we shall not succeed in eliminating it systematically and radically, unless we emphasize more and pay greater honor, before everyone's eyes, in the sight of every society, to *the second dimension of the goods of man:* the dimension that does not divide people but puts them into communication with each other, associates them and unites them.

I consider that the famous opening words of the Charter of the United Nations, in which "the peoples of the United Nations, determined to save succeeding generations from the scourge of war" solemnly reaffirmed "faith in fundamental human rights, in the dignity and worth of the human person, in the equal rights of men and women and of nations large and small," are meant to stress this dimension.

Indeed, the fight against incipient wars cannot be carried out on a merely superficial level, by treating the symptoms. It must be done in a radical way, by attacking the causes. The reason I have called attention to the dimension constituted by spiritual realities is my concern for the cause of peace, peace which is built up by men and women uniting around what is most fully and profoundly human, around what raises them above the world about them and determines their indestructible grandeur—indestructible in spite of the death to which everyone on earth is subject. I would like to add that *the Catholic Church* and, I think I can say, the whole of Christianity sees in this very domain *its own particular task.* The Second Vatican Council helped to establish what the Christian faith has in common with the various non-Christian religions in this aspiration. The Church is therefore grateful to all who show respect and good will with regard to this mission of hers and do not impede it or make it difficult. An analysis of the history of mankind, especially at its present stage, shows how important is the duty of revealing more fully the range of the goods that are linked with the spiritual dimension of human existence. It shows how important this task is for building peace and how serious is any threat to human rights. Any violation of them; even in a "peace situation," is a form of warfare against humanity.

It seems that in the modern world there are two main threats. Both concern human rights in the field of international relations and human rights within the individual States or societies.

17. The first of these systematic threats against human rights is linked in an overall sense with the distribution of material goods. This distribution is frequently unjust both within individual societies and on the planet as a whole. Everyone knows that these goods are given to man not only as nature's bounty: they are enjoyed by him chiefly as the fruit of his

many activities, ranging from the simplest manual and physical labor to the most complicated forms of industrial production, and to the highly qualified and specialized research and study. Various forms of *inequality in the possession of material goods,* and in the enjoyment of them, can often be explained by different historical and cultural causes and circumstances. But, while these circumstances can diminish the moral responsibility of people today, they do not prevent the situations of inequality from being marked by injustice and social injury.

People must become aware that economic tensions within countries and in the relationship between States and even between entire continents contain within themselves substantial elements that restrict or violate human rights. Such elements are the exploitation of labor and many other abuses that affect the dignity of the human person. It follows that the fundamental criterion for comparing social, economic and political systems is not, *and cannot be,* the criterion of hegemony and imperialism: it can be, and indeed it must be, *the humanistic criterion,* namely, the measure in which each system is really capable of reducing, restraining and eliminating as far as possible the various forms of exploitation of man and of ensuring for him, through work, not only the just distribution of the indispensable material goods, but also a participation, in keeping with his dignity, in the whole process of production and in the social life that grows up around that process. Let us not forget that, although man depends on the resources of the material world for his life, he cannot be their slave, but he must be their master. The words of the book of Genesis, "Fill the earth and subdue it" (Gn. 1:28), are in a sense a primary and essential directive in the field of economy and of labor policy.

18. Humanity as a whole, and the individual nations, have certainly made remarkable progress in this field during the last hundred years. But it is a field in which there is never any lack of systematic threats and violations of human rights. Disturbing factors are frequently present in the form of the *frightful disparities* between excessively rich individuals and groups on the one hand, and on the other hand *the majority* made up of the poor or indeed of *the destitute,* who lack food and opportunities for work and education and are in great numbers condemned to hunger and disease. And concern is also caused at times by the radical separation of work from property, by man's indifference to the production enterprise to which he is linked only by a work obligation, without feeling that he is working for a good that will be his or for himself.

It is no secret that the abyss separating the minority of the excessively rich from the multitude of the destitute is a very grave symptom in the life of any society. This must also be said with even greater insistence with regard to the abyss separating countries and regions of the earth. Surely the only way to overcome this serious disparity between areas of satiety and areas of hunger and depression is through coordinated cooperation by all countries. This requires above all else a unity inspired by an authentic perspective of peace. Everything will depend on whether these differences and contrasts in the sphere of the "possession" of goods will be systematically reduced through truly effective means, on whether the belts of hunger, malnutrition, destitution, underdevelopment, disease and illiteracy will disappear from the economic map of the earth, and on whether peaceful cooperation will avoid imposing conditions of exploitation and economic or political dependence, which would only be a form of neocolonialism.

19. I would now like to draw attention to *a second systematic threat* to man in his inalienable rights in the modern world, a threat which constitutes no less a danger than the first to the cause of peace. I refer to the various forms of injustice in the field of the spirit.

Man can indeed be wounded in his inner relationship with truth, in his conscience, in his most personal belief, in his view of the world, in his religious faith, and in the sphere of what are known as civil liberties. Decisive for these last is equality of rights without discrimination on grounds of origin, race, sex, nationality, religion, political convictions and the like. Equality of rights means the exclusion of the various forms of privilege for some and discrimination against others, whether they are people born in the same country or people from different backgrounds of history, nationality, race and ideology. For centuries the thrust of civilization has been in one direction: that of giving the life of individual political societies a form in which there can be *fully safeguarded the objective rights of the spirit, of human conscience and of human creativity, including man's relationship with God.* Yet in spite of this we still see in this field recurring threats and violations, often with no possibility of appealing to a higher authority or of obtaining an effective remedy.

Besides the acceptance of legal formulas safeguarding the principle of the freedom of the human spirit, such as freedom of thought and expression, religious freedom, and freedom of conscience, structures of social life often exist in which the practical exercise of these freedoms condemns man, in fact if not formally, to become a second-class or third-class citizen, to see compromised his chances of social advancement, his professional career or his access to certain posts of responsibility, and to lose even the possibility of educating his children freely. It is a question of the highest importance that in internal social life, as well as in international life, *all human beings* in every nation and country *should be able to enjoy effectively their full rights under any political regime or system.*

Only the safeguarding of this real completeness of rights for every human being without discrimination can ensure peace at its very roots.

20. With regard to religious freedom, which I, as Pope, am bound to have particularly at heart, precisely with a view to safeguarding peace, I would like to repeat here, as a contribution to respect for man's spiritual dimension, some principles contained in the Second Vatican Council's Declaration *Dignitatis humanae:* "In accordance with their dignity, all human beings, because they are persons, that is, beings endowed with reason and free will and therefore bearing personal responsibility, are both impelled by their nature and bound by a moral obligation to seek the truth, especially religious truth. They are also bound to adhere to the truth once they come to know it and to direct their whole lives in accordance with its demands" *(Dignitatis humanae, 2).*

"The practice of religion of its very nature consists primarily of those voluntary and free internal acts by which a human being directly sets his course towards God. No merely human power can either command or prohibit acts of this kind. But man's social nature itself requires that he give external expression to his internal acts of religion, that he communicate with others in religious matters and that he profess his religion in community'' *(Dignitatis humanae*, 3).

These words touch the very substance of the question. They also show how even the confrontation between *the religious view of the world and the agnostic or even atheistic view,* which is one of the ''signs of the times'' of the present age, could preserve honest and respectful human dimensions without violating the essential rights of conscience of any man or woman living on earth.

Respect for the dignity of the human person would seem to demand that, when the exact tenor of the exercise of religious freedom is being discussed or determined with a view to national laws or international conventions, the institutions that are by their nature at the service of religion should also be brought in. If this participation is omitted, there is a danger of imposing, in so intimate a field of man's life, rules or restrictions that are opposed to his true religious needs.

21. The United Nations Organization has proclaimed *1979 the Year of the Child.* In the presence of the representatives of so many nations of the world gathered here, I wish to express the joy that we all find in children, the springtime of life, the anticipation of the future history of each of our present earthly homelands. No country on earth, no political system can think of its own future otherwise than

through the image of these new generations that will receive from their parents the manifold heritage of values, duties and aspirations of the nation to which they belong and of the whole human family. Concern for the child, even before birth, from the first moment of conception and then throughout the years of infancy and youth, is the primary and fundamental test of the relationship of one human being to another.

And so, what better wish can I express for every nation and the whole of mankind, and for all the children of the world than *a better future* in which respect for human rights will become a complete reality throughout the third millennium, which is drawing near.

22. But in this perspective we must ask ourselves whether there will continue to accumulate over the heads of this new generation of children the threat of common extermination for which the means are in the hands of the modern States, especially the major world powers. *Are the children to receive the arms race from us* as a necessary inheritance? How are we to explain this unbridled race?

The ancients said: *Si vis pacem, para bellum.* But can our age still really believe that the breathtaking spiral of armaments is at the service of world peace? In alleging the threat of a potential enemy, is it really not rather the intention to keep for oneself a means of threat, in order to get the upper hand with the aid of one's own arsenal of destruction? Here too it is the human dimension of peace that tends to vanish *in favor of ever new possible forms of imperialism.*

It must be our solemn wish here for our children, for the children of all the nations on earth, that this point will never be reached. And for that reason I do

not cease to pray to God each day so that in His mercy He may save us from so terrible a day.

23. At the close of this address, I wish to express once more before all the high representatives of the States who are present a word of esteem and deep love for all the peoples, all the nations of the earth, for all human communities. Each one has its own history and culture. I hope that they will live and grow in the freedom and truth of their own history. For that is the measure of the common good of each one of them. I hope that each person will *live and grow strong with the moral force of the community* that forms its members as citizens. I hope that the State authorities, while respecting the just rights of each citizen, will enjoy the confidence of all for the common good. I hope that all the nations, even the smallest, even those that do not yet enjoy full sovereignty, and those that have been forcibly robbed of it, will meet in full equality with the others in the United Nations Organization. I hope that the United Nations will ever remain the supreme forum of peace and justice, the authentic seat of freedom of peoples and individuals in their longing for a better future.

PEACE, ORDER, JUSTICE AND PROGRESS FOR ALL

Having delivered his message to the United Nations General Assembly, the Holy Father met the diplomats to whom he spoke in French. Following this he met the directors of the Intergovernmental and Non-governmental Organizations at the U.N. Headquarters and spoke to them as follows:

Ladies and Gentlemen,

It gives me great pleasure to extend my greetings to the representatives of the intergovernmental and non-governmental organizations who are here present, and to thank you for your cordial welcome.

Your presence at the center of the United Nations' activities is a consequence of the growing awareness that the problems of today's world can only be solved when all forces are joined together and directed towards the same common aim. The problems that the human family faces today may seem overwhelming. I for my part am convinced that there is immense potential with which to face them. History tells us that the human race is capable of reacting and of changing direction every time it perceives clearly the warning that it is on the wrong course. You are privileged to witness in this building how the Representatives of the nations endeavor to chart a common course in order that life on this planet will be lived in peace, order, justice and progress for all. But you are also aware that every individual must work towards the same end. It is individual actions put together which bring about today and tomorrow the total impact which is either beneficial or harmful for humanity.

The various programs and organizations that exist within the framework of the United Nations Organization, as well as the Specialized Agencies and other intergovernmental bodies, are an important part of that total effort. In the area of its own specialization—be it food, agriculture, trade, environment, development, science, culture, education, health, disaster relief, or the problems of children and refugees—each one of these organizations makes a unique contribution not only to providing for people's wants, but also to fostering respect for human dignity and the cause of world peace.

No organization, however, not even the United Nations or any of its specialized agencies, can alone solve the global problems which are constantly brought to its attention, if its concerns are not shared by all the people. It is then the privileged task of the non-governmental organizations to help bring these concerns into the communities and the homes of the people, and to bring back to the established agencies the priorities and aspirations of the people, so that all the solutions and projects which are envisaged be truly geared to the needs of the human person.

The Delegates who drafted the Charter of the United Nations had a vision of united and cooperating governments, but behind the nations, they saw also the individual and they wanted every human being to be free and to enjoy his or her fundamental rights. This fundamental inspiration must be preserved.

I wish to express my best wishes to all of you here who work together to bring the benefits of concerted action to all parts of the world. My cordial greeting goes to the Representatives of the various Protestant, Jewish and Moslem associations, and in a particular way to the Representatives of the International Catholic Organizations. May your dedication and your moral sense never become blunted by difficulties; may you never lose sight of the ultimate aim of your efforts: to create a world where every human person can live in dignity and loving harmony as a child of God.

HAVE CONFIDENCE IN THE IDEAL YOU SERVE

While visiting the United Nations the Holy Father met the members of the staff of the Organization and delivered the following discourse.

Ladies and gentlemen, dear friends,

It is with great pleasure that I take this opportunity to greet all the members of the staff of the United Nations Headquarters in New York, and to reiterate before you my firm belief in the extraordinary value and importance of the role and activities of this international institution, of all its agencies and programs.

When you accepted to serve here, either in study or research, in administrative tasks or in planning, in secretarial or logistical activities, you did so because you believed that your work, often hidden and unnoticed in the complexity of this operation, would constitute a valuable contribution to the aims and objectives of this Organization. And rightly so, for the first time in the history of humanity, there exists the possibility for all peoples, through their representatives, to meet constantly with each other in order to exchange views; to confer on and to seek peaceful solutions, effective solutions to the conflicts and problems that are causing suffering in all parts of the world to large numbers of men, women and children. You are part of this great and universal endeavor. You provide the necessary services, information and help that are indispensable for the success of this exciting adventure—you guarantee continuity of action and implementation. Each one of you is a servant of the unity, peace and brotherhood of all men.

Your task is not less important than that of the representatives of the nations of the world, provided you are motivated by the great ideal of world peace and fraternal collaboration between all peoples: what counts is the spirit with which you perform your tasks. Peace and harmony among the nations, the progress of all humanity, the possibility for all men and women to live in dignity and happiness depend on you, on each one of you, and on the tasks that you perform here.

The builders of the pyramids in Egypt and Mexico, of the temples of Asia, of the cathedrals in Europe were not only the architects who laid out the designs, or those who provided financing, but also, and in no small way, the carvers of the stones, many of whom never had the satisfaction of contemplating in its entirety the beauty of the masterpiece that their hands helped create. And yet, they were producing a work of art that would be the object of admiration for generations to come.

You are in so many ways the carvers of the stones. Even a lifetime of dedicated service will not always enable you to see the finished monument of universal peace, of fraternal collaboration and of true harmony between peoples. Sometimes you will catch a glimpse of it, in a particularly successful achievement, in a problem solved, in the smile of a happy and healthy child, in a conflict avoided, in a reconciliation of minds and hearts achieved. More often, you will experience only the monotony of your daily labors, or the frustrations of bureaucratic entanglements. But know that your work is great and that history will judge your achievements with favor. The challenges that the world community will face in the coming years and decades will not diminish. The rapidly changing pace of world events, the tremendous steps forward of science and technology will increase both the potential for development and the complexity of the problems. Be prepared, be capable, but above all have confidence in the ideal you serve.

Look upon your contribution not only in terms of increased industrial production, of enhanced efficiency, of eliminated suffering. Above all, look upon it in terms of growing dignity for every human being, of increased possibility for every person to advance to the fullest measure of spiritual, cultural and human completion. Your calling as international servants takes its value from the objectives pursued by the international organizations. These aims transcend the mere material or intellectual spheres; they reach out into the moral and spiritual fields. Through your work, you are able to extend your love to the entire human family, to every person who has received the wondrous gift of life, so that all may live together in peace and harmony, in a just and peaceful world, where all their basic needs—physical, moral and spiritual—may be fulfilled.

You have in the visitor who stands before you someone who admires what you do and who believes in the value of your task.

Thank you for your welcome. I send my heartfelt greetings also to your families. I especially hope that you may experience a deep and never fading joy in the work that you perform for the benefit of all men, women and children on this earth.

SERVANTS OF TRUTH

To the journalists accredited to the United Nations, the Holy Father, in the late afternoon of October 2, gave the following address:

My dear friends of the communications media,

It would hardly be possible for me to depart from the United Nations without saying "thank you" from my heart to those who have reported, not only this day's events, but all the activities of this worthy organization. In this international assembly, you can truly be instruments of peace by being messengers of truth.

You are indeed servants of truth; you are its tireless transmitters, diffusers, defenders. You are dedicated communicators, promoting unity among all nations by sharing truth among all peoples.

If your reporting does not always command the attention you would desire, or if it does not always conclude with the success that you would wish, do not grow discouraged. Be faithful to the truth and to its transmission, for truth endures; truth will not go away. Truth will not pass or change.

And I say to you—take it as my parting word to you—that the service of truth, the service of humanity through the medium of the truth, is something worthy of your best years, your finest talents, your most dedicated efforts. As transmitters of truth, you are instruments of understanding among people and of peace among nations.

May God bless your labors for truth with the fruit of peace. This is my prayer for you, for your families and for those whom you serve as messengers of truth, and as instruments of peace.

MY PEACE I LEAVE YOU, MY PEACE I GIVE YOU!

Having expressed his thanks to the representatives of the nations and the Secretariat of the United Nations, Pope John Paul spoke his farewell message in the following discourse.

Mr. Secretary-General,

As I am about to conclude my all too brief visit at the world headquarters of the United Nations, I wish to express my heartfelt thanks to all who were instrumental in making this visit possible.

My thanks go first of all to you, Mr. Secretary-General, for your kind invitation, which I considered not only a great honor but also an obligation, since it allowed me by my presence here to attest publicly and solemnly to the commitment of the Holy See to collaborate, to the extent consonant with its own mission, with this worthy Organization.

My gratitude goes also to the distinguished President of the Thirty-fourth General Assembly, who honored me in inviting me to address this unique forum of the delegates of nearly all the nations of the world. By proclaiming the incomparable dignity of every human being and by manifesting my firm belief in the unity and solidarity of all nations, I have been permitted to affirm once again a basic tenet of my encyclical letter: "After all, peace comes down to respect for man's inviolable rights" *(Redemptor hominis,* 17).

May I also thank all the distinguished delegates of the nations represented here, as well as the whole staff of the United Nations, for the friendly reception

which they have given to the representatives of the
Holy See, particularly to our Permanent Observer,
Archbishop Giovanni Cheli.

The message which I wish to leave with you is a
message of certitude and hope: the certitude that
peace is possible when it is based on the recognition
of the fatherhood of God and the brotherhood of all
men; the hope that the sense of moral responsibility
which every person must assume will make it possible to create a better world in freedom, in justice and
in love.

As one whose ministry is void of meaning except
insofar as he is the faithful Vicar of Christ on earth, I
now take leave of you with the words of the one
whom I represent, of Jesus Christ Himself: "Peace I
leave with you, my peace I give to you" (Jn. 14:27).
My constant prayer for all of you is this: that there
may be peace in justice and in love. May the praying
voice of all those who believe in God—Christians and
non-Christians alike—bring it about that the moral
resources present in the hearts of men and women of
good will be united for the common good, and call
down from heaven that peace which human efforts
alone cannot effect.

May God bless the United Nations.

DIRECT MAN'S GAZE TOWARDS THE MYSTERY OF CHRIST

After his visit to the United Nations, the Holy Father went to St. Patrick's Cathedral where an immense crowd was waiting. After an address of welcome by Terence Cardinal Cooke, Archbishop of New York, Pope John Paul II delivered the following address.

Dear Cardinal Cooke, dear brothers and sisters in Christ,

I consider it a special grace to come back to New York—to be back in St. Patrick's during the Cathedral's centenary year.

Six months ago I wrote a letter to Cardinal Cooke, stating that it was "my earnest hope that the local ecclesial community, symbolized by this glorious edifice in stone (cf. 1 Pt. 2:5), may be renewed in the faith of Peter and Paul—in the faith of our Lord Jesus Christ—and that each one of you will find fresh vigor for authentic Christian living." And this is my hope for all of you today. This is why I am here: to confirm you in your holy, Catholic and apostolic faith; to invoke upon you the joy and strength that will sustain you in Christian living.

On this occasion I send my greetings to all the people of New York. In a special way my heart is with the poor, with those who suffer, with those who are alone and abandoned in the midst of this teeming metropolis.

I pray for the success of the apostolate in this archdiocese: May the spires of St. Patrick's Cathedral always reflect the thrust with which the Church fulfills her fundamental function in every age: "To direct man's gaze, to point the awareness and experience of the whole of humanity towards the mystery of Christ, to help all men and women to be familiar with the profundity of the redemption taking place in Christ Jesus" *(Redemptor hominis,* 10).

This too is included in the symbolism of Saint Patrick's; this is the mission of the Church in New York—the expression of her vital and distinctive service to humanity: to direct hearts to God, to keep alive hope in the world. And so we repeat with Saint Paul: "This explains why we work and struggle as we do; our hopes are fixed on the living God" (Tm. 4:10).

"WE ARE EASTER PEOPLE..."

En route to Yankee Stadium, the Holy Father stopped in the two quarters of Harlem and South Bronx, inhabited principally by the Blacks and Puerto Ricans respectively. At Harlem in front of the Church of St. Charles Borromeo, the Pope listened to an address of welcome and then spoke as follows:

Dear friends, dear brothers and sisters in Christ,

"This is the day the Lord has made; let us be glad and rejoice in it" (Ps. 118:24).

I greet you in the joy and peace of our Lord Jesus Christ. I welcome this opportunity to be with you and to speak to you, and through you to extend my greetings to all black Americans.

At Cardinal Cooke's suggestion, I was happy to include in my plans a visit to the parish of St. Charles Borromeo in Harlem, and to its black community, which for half a century has nurtured here the cultural, social and religious roots of black people. I have greatly looked forward to being here this evening.

I come to you as a servant of Jesus Christ, and I want to speak to you about Him. Christ came to bring joy: joy to children, joy to parents, joy to families and to friends, joy to workers and to scholars, joy to the sick and to the elderly, joy to all humanity. In a true sense, joy is the keynote of the Christian message and the recurring motif of the Gospels. Recall the first words of the angel to Mary: "Rejoice, O full of grace, the Lord is with you" (Lk. 1:28). And at the birth

of Jesus, the angels announced to the shepherds: "Listen, I bring you news of great joy, joy to be shared by all people" (Lk.2:10). Years later as Jesus entered Jerusalem riding on a colt, "the whole group of disciples joyfully began to praise God at the top of their voices. 'Blessed is the king who comes in the name of the Lord'!" (Lk. 19:37-38) We are told that some pharisees in the crowd complained, saying: "Master, stop your disciples." But Jesus answered: "I tell you, if they were silent, the very stones would cry out" (Lk. 19:39-40).

Are not those words of Jesus still true today? If we are silent about the joy that comes from knowing Jesus, the very stones of our cities will cry out! For we are an Easter people and "Alleluia" is our song. With St. Paul I exhort you: "Rejoice in the Lord always, I say it again, rejoice" (Phil. 4:4).

Rejoice because Jesus has come into the world!

Rejoice because Jesus has died upon the cross!

Rejoice because He rose again from the dead!

Rejoice because in Baptism, He washed away our sins!

Rejoice because Jesus has come to set us free!

And rejoice because He is the Master of our life!

But how many people have never known this joy? They feed on emptiness and tread the paths of despair. "They walk in darkness and the shadow of death" (Lk. 1:79). And we need not look to the far ends of the earth for them. They live in our neighborhoods, they walk down our streets, they may even be members of our own families. They live without true joy because they live without hope. They live without hope because they have never heard, really heard the Good News of Jesus Christ, because they have never met a brother or a sister who touched their lives with the love of Jesus and lifted them up from their misery.

We must go to them therefore as messengers of hope. We must bring to them the witness of true joy. We must pledge to them our commitment to work for a just society and city where they feel respected and loved.

And so I encourage you, be men and women of deep and abiding faith. Be heralds of hope. Be messengers of joy. Be true workers for justice. Let the Good News of Christ radiate from your hearts, and the peace He alone gives remain forever in your souls.

My dear brothers and sisters in the black community: "Rejoice in the Lord always, again I say rejoice."

THAT THE FLAME
OF HOPE MIGHT
GROW BRIGHTER

To a large group of Spanish-speaking immigrants who had gathered on the corner of Morris Avenue and 152nd Street, the Holy Father spoke in Spanish. A translation follows.

Dear brothers and sisters and friends,

One of the visits to which I attribute great importance, and to which I would like to be able to devote more time, is precisely the one that I am now making to South Bronx, in this immense city of New York, where many immigrants of different colors, races and peoples live, among them the numerous Spanish-speaking community, you, to whom I am now addressing myself.

I come here because I know of the difficult conditions of your existence, because I know that your lives are marked by pain. For this reason you deserve special attention on the part of the Pope.

My presence in this place is meant to be a sign of gratitude and as an encouragement for what the Church has done and is continuing to do, through her parishes, schools, health centers, institutes for assisting youth and the aging, on behalf of so many who experience inner anxiety and material deprivation.

I would wish that this flame of hope—sometimes one of the least hopes—should not only not go out, but that it might increase in strength, so that all who live in the area and the city may succeed in being able to live with dignity and serenity, as individual human beings, as families, as sons and daughters of God.

Brothers and sisters and friends, do not give in to despair, but work together, take the steps possible for you in the task of increasing your dignity, unite your efforts towards the goals of human and moral advancement. And do not forget that God has your lives in His care, goes with you, calls you to better things, calls you to overcome.

But since help from outside is also necessary, I make an insistent call to the leaders, to those who can do it, that they should give their generous collaboration in such a praiseworthy and urgent task.

Please God that the house-building project—and other necessary projects—may soon become a beautiful reality, so that each person and each family may find suitable housing in which to live in peace beneath the gaze of God.

Friends, I greet you and all those dear to you, I bless you and I encourage you not to grow faint as you travel the right road.

OPEN WIDE THE DOORS FOR CHRIST

To some 80,000 faithful of New York gathered in Yankee Stadium on the evening of October 2, Pope John Paul, after the Gospel of the Mass, delivered the following homily.

1. "Peace be with you!"

These were the first words that Jesus spoke to His apostles after His resurrection. With these words the risen Christ restored peace to their hearts, at a time when they were still in a state of shock after the first terrible experience of Good Friday. Tonight, in the name of our Lord Jesus Christ, in the power of His spirit, in the midst of a world that is anxious about its own existence, I repeat these words to you, for they are words of life: "Peace be with you!"

Jesus does not merely give us peace. He gives us *His* peace accompanied by *His* justice. He *is* peace and justice. He becomes *our* peace and *our* justice.

What does this mean? It means that Jesus Christ —the Son of God made man, the perfect man—perfects, restores and manifests in Himself the unsurpassable dignity that God wishes to give to man from the beginning. He is the one who realizes in Himself what man has the vocation to be: the one who is fully reconciled with the Father, fully one in Himself, fully devoted to others. Jesus Christ is living peace and living justice.

Jesus Christ makes us sharers in what He is. Through His incarnation, the Son of God in a certain manner united Himself with every human being. In our inmost being He has recreated us; in our inmost being He has reconciled us with God, reconciled us with ourselves, reconciled us with our brothers and sisters: He is *our* peace.

2. What unfathomable riches we bear within us, and in our Christian communities! We are bearers of the justice and peace of God! We are not primarily painstaking builders of a justice and peace that are merely human, always wearing out and always fragile. We are primarily the humble beneficiaries of the very life of God, who is justice and peace in the bond of charity. During Mass, when the priest greets us with these words: "The peace of the Lord be with you always," let us think primarily of this peace which is God's gift: Jesus Christ our peace. And when, before Communion, the priest invites us to give one another a sign of peace, let us think primarily of the fact that we are invited to exchange with one another the peace of Christ who dwells within us, who invites us to share in His Body and Blood, for our joy and for the service of all humanity.

For God's justice and peace cry out to bear fruit in human works of justice and peace, in all the spheres of actual life. When we Christians make Jesus Christ the center of our feelings and thoughts, we do not turn away from people and their needs. On the contrary, we are caught up in the eternal movement of God's love that comes to meet us; we are caught up in the movement of the Son, who came among us, who became one of us; we are caught up in the movement of the Holy Spirit, who visits the poor, calms fevered hearts, binds up wounded hearts, warms cold hearts, and gives us the fullness of His gifts. The reason why man is the primary and fundamental way for the

Church is that the Church walks in the footsteps of Jesus: it is Jesus who has shown her this road. This road passes in an unchangeable way through the mystery of the Incarnation and Redemption; it leads from Christ to man. The Church looks at the world through the very eyes of Christ; Jesus is the principle of the solicitude for man (cf. *Redemptor hominis*, 13-18).

3. The task is immense. And it is an enthralling one. I have just emphasized various aspects of it before the General Assembly of the United Nations, and I shall touch upon others during my apostolic journey across your country. Today, let me just dwell on the spirit and nature of the Church's contribution to the cause of justice and peace, and let me also mention certain urgent priorities which your service to humanity ought to concentrate upon today.

Social thinking and social practice inspired by the Gospel must always be marked by a special sensitivity towards those who are most in distress, those who are extremely poor, those suffering from all the physical, mental and moral ills that afflict humanity, including hunger, neglect, unemployment and despair. There many poor people of this sort around the world. There are many in your own midst. On many occasions, your nation has gained a well-deserved reputation for generosity, both public and private. Be faithful to that tradition, in keeping with your vast possibilities and present responsibilities. The network of charitable works of each kind that the Church has succeeded in creating here is a valuable means for effectively mobilizing generous undertakings aimed at relieving the situations of distress that continually arise both at home and elsewhere in the world. Make

To all, I have come with a message of hope and peace—the hope and peace of Jesus Christ, for whom every human being is of immense value and dignity, and in whom are found all the treasures of justice and love.

To all I want to say how happy I am to be in your midst. I pray for each one of you, asking you to remain always united in Jesus Christ and His Church, so that together we may "display to the world our unity in proclaiming the mystery of Christ...."

From so many quarters—Catholics, Protestants and Jews—America has opened her heart to me. And on my part I come to you—America—with sentiments of friendship, reverence and esteem. I come as one who already knows you and loves you, as one who wishes you to fulfill completely your noble destiny of service to the world.

And to all of you, the laity, I open my heart in love and trust. You are the workers for evangelization in the realities of daily life, and you give witness to the love of Christ in the service that you give to all your fellow men and women, beginning with your own families.

I have come to America to call you to Christ—to call all of you and each of you to live in His love, today and forever!

I wish to state again how greatly I value your Institution. For as I stated on that other occasion: ''You are the first to be convinced that there can be no true human progress or lasting peace without the courageous, loyal and disinterested pursuit of growing cooperation and unity among people.''

Arturo Mari

I greet all the men, women and children of the countries that are represented at the United Nations. May the
hopes that they place in the efforts and in the solidarity
that link us all never be disappointed. May they experience in the achievements of the United Nations the
fact that there is only one world, and that it is the home
of all.

I would like to express the wish that, in view of its universal character, the United Nations Organization will never cease to be the forum, the high tribune from which all man's problems are appraised in truth and justice.

I greet all Americans without distinction; I want to meet you and tell you all—men and women of all creeds and ethnic origins, children and youth, fathers and mothers, the sick and the elderly—that God loves you, that He has given you a dignity as human beings that is beyond compare. I want to tell everyone that the Pope is your friend and a servant of your humanity.

Arturo Mari

Christ came to bring joy: joy to children, joy to parents, joy to families and to friends, joy to workers and to scholars, joy to the sick and to the elderly, joy to all humanity.

Let the Good News of Christ radiate from your hearts, and the peace He alone gives remain forever in your souls.

What unfathomable riches we bear within us, and in our Christian communities! We are bearers of the justice and peace of God! We are not primarily painstaking builders of a justice and peace that are merely human, always wearing out and always fragile. We are primarily the humble beneficiaries of the very life of God, who is justice and peace in the bond of charity.

Arturo Mari

With deep conviction and affection I repeat to you:
"Do not be afraid. Open wide the doors for Christ. To His
saving power open the boundaries of states, economic
and political systems, the vast fields of culture, civilization and development. Do not be afraid. Christ knows
what is in man. He alone knows it."

Arturo Mari

When we Christians make Jesus Christ the center of our feelings and thoughts, we do not turn away from people and their needs. On the contrary, we are caught up in the eternal movement of God's love that comes to meet us.

This is what education is all about, this is the meaning of life: to know Christ. To know Christ as a friend: as someone who cares about you and the person next to you, and all the people here and everywhere—no matter what language they speak, or what clothes they wear, or what color their skin is.

Arturo Mari

We have to learn to meet challenges and even crises in the light of Christ's cross and resurrection. Part of our Catholic education is to learn to see the needs of others, to have the courage to practice what we believe in.

Arturo Mari

Dear young people: by a real Christian life, by the practice of your religion you are called to give witness to your faith. And because actions speak louder than words, you are called to proclaim, by the conduct of your daily lives, that you really do believe that Jesus Christ is Lord!

an effort to ensure that this form of aid keeps its ir-replaceable character as a fraternal and personal encounter with those who are in distress; if neces-sary, re-establish this very character against all the elements that work in the opposite direction. Let this sort of aid be respectful of the freedom and dignity of those being helped, and let it be a means of forming the conscience of the givers.

4. But this is not enough. Within the framework of your national institutions and in cooperation with all your compatriots, you will also want to seek out the structural reasons which foster or cause the dif-ferent forms of poverty in the world and in your own country, so that you can apply the proper remedies. You will not allow yourselves to be intimidated or discouraged by over-simplified explanations, which are more ideological than scientific explanations which try to account for a complex evil by some single cause. But neither will you recoil before the reforms—even profound ones—of attitudes and struc-tures that may prove necessary in order to recreate over and over again the conditions needed by the disadvantaged if they are to have a fresh chance in the hard struggle of life. The poor of the United States and of the world are your brothers and sisters in Christ. You must never be content to leave them just the crumbs from the feast. You must take of your sub-stance, and not just of your abundance, in order to help them. And you must treat them like guests at your family table.

5. Catholics of the United States, while develop-ing your own legitimate institutions, you also par-ticipate in the nation's affairs within the framework of institutions and organizations springing from the

nation's common history and from your common concern. This you do hand in hand with your fellow citizens of every creed and confession. Unity among you in all such endeavors is essential, under the leadership of your Bishops, for deepening, proclaiming and effectively promoting the truth about man, his dignity and his inalienable rights, the truth such as the Church receives it in revelation and such as she ceaselessly develops it in her social teaching in the light of the Gospel. These shared convictions, however, are not a ready-made model for society (cf. *Octogesima adveniens*, 42). It is principally the task of lay people to put them into practice in concrete projects, to define priorities and to develop models that are suitable for promoting man's real good. The Second Vatican Council's Pastoral Constitution *Gaudium et spes* tells us that "lay people should seek from priests light and spiritual strength. Let the lay people not imagine that their pastors are always such experts, that to every problem which arises, however complicated, they can readily give a concrete solution, or even that such is their mission. Rather, enlightened by Christian wisdom and giving close attention to the teaching authority of the Church, let the lay people assume their own distinctive role" (*Gaudium et spes*, 43).

6. In order to bring this undertaking to a successful conclusion, fresh spiritual and moral energy drawn from the inexhaustible divine source is needed. This energy does not develop easily. The life-style of many of the members of our rich and permissive societies is easy, and so is the life-style of increasing groups inside the poorer countries. As I said last year to the plenary assembly of the Pontifical Commission

Justice and Peace, "Christians will want to be in the vanguard in favoring ways of life that decisively break with the frenzy of consumerism, exhausting and joyless" (Nov. 11, 1978). It is not a question of slowing down progress, for there is no human progress when everything conspires to give full reign to the instincts of self-interest, sex and power. We must find a simple way of living. For it is not right that the standard of living of the rich countries should seek to maintain itself by draining off a great part of the reserves of energy and raw materials that are meant to serve the whole of humanity. For readiness to create a greater and more equitable solidarity between peoples is the first condition for peace. Catholics of the United States, and all you citizens of the United States, you have such a tradition of spiritual generosity, industry, simplicity and sacrifice that you cannot fail to heed this call today for a new enthusiasm and a fresh determination. It is in the joyful simplicity of a life inspired by the Gospel and the Gospel's spirit of fraternal sharing that you will find the best remedy for sour criticism, paralyzing doubt and the temptation to make money the principal means and indeed the very measure of human advancement.

On various occasions, I have referred to the Gospel parable of the rich man and Lazarus. "Once there was a rich man who dressed in purple and linen and feasted splendidly every day. At his gate lay a beggar named Lazarus who was covered with sores. Lazarus longed to eat the scraps that fell from the rich man's table" (Lk. 16:19ff.). Both the rich man and the beggar died and were carried before Abraham, and there judgment was rendered on their conduct. And the Scripture tells us that Lazarus found consolation, but that the rich man found torment. Was the rich man condemned because he had riches, because he abounded in earthly possessions, because he "dressed in purple linen and feasted splendidly every day"? No, I would say that it was not for this reason. The rich man was condemned because he did not pay attention to the other man. Because he failed to take notice of Lazarus, the person who sat at his door and who longed to eat the scraps from his table. Nowhere does Christ condemn the mere possession of earthly goods as such. Instead, He pronounces very harsh words against those who use their possessions in a selfish way, without paying attention to the needs of others. The Sermon on the Mount begins with the words: "Blessed are the poor in spirit." And at the end of the account of the Last Judgment as found in St. Matthew's Gospel, Jesus speaks the words that we all know so well: "I was hungry and you gave me no food, I was thirsty and you gave me no drink. I was away from home and you gave me no welcome, naked and you gave me no clothing. I was ill and in prison and you did not come and comfort me" (Mt. 25:42-43).

The parable of the rich man and Lazarus must always be present in our memory; it must form our conscience. Christ demands openness to our brothers and sisters in need—openness from the rich, the affluent, the economically advanced; openness to the poor, the underdeveloped and the disadvantaged. Christ demands an openness that is more than benign attention, more than token actions or half-hearted efforts that leave the poor as destitute as before or even more so.

All of humanity must think of the parable of the rich man and the beggar. Humanity must translate it into contemporary terms, in terms of economy and politics, in terms of all human rights, in terms of relations between the "First," "Second," and "Third World." We cannot stand idly by when thousands of human beings are dying of hunger. Nor can we remain indifferent when the rights of the human spirit are trampled upon, when violence is done to the human conscience in matters of truth, religion, and cultural creativity.

We cannot stand idly by, enjoying our own riches and freedom, if, in any place, the Lazarus of the twentieth century stands at our doors. In the light of the parable of Christ, riches and freedom mean a special responsibility. Riches and freedom create a special obligation. And so, in the name of the solidarity that binds us all together in a common humanity, I again proclaim the dignity of every human person: the rich man and Lazarus are both human beings, both of them equally created in the image and likeness of God, both of them equally redeemed by Christ, at a great price, the price of "the precious blood of Christ" (1 Pt. 1:19).

Brothers and sisters in Christ, with deep conviction and affection I repeat to you the words that I addressed to the world when I took up my apostolic ministry in the service of all men and women: "Do not be afraid. Open wide the doors for Christ. To His saving power open the boundaries of states, economic and political systems, the vast fields of culture, civilization and development. Do not be afraid. Christ knows what is in man. He alone knows it" (Oct. 22, 1978).

As I said to you at the beginning, Christ is our justice and our peace, and all our works of justice and peace draw from this source the irreplaceable energy and light for the great task before us. As we resolutely commit ourselves to the service of all the needs of individuals and of peoples—for Christ urges us to do so—we shall nevertheless remind ourselves that the Church's mission is not limited to this witness to social fruitfulness of the Gospel. Along this road that leads the Church to man, she does not offer, in the matter of justice and peace, only the earthly fruits of the Gospel; she brings to man—to every human person—their very source: Jesus Christ Himself, our justice and our peace.

WHO WILL SEPARATE US FROM CHRIST?

In the course of morning prayer in St. Patrick's Cathedral, on October 3, in the presence of numerous Bishops, priests, religious, seminarians, laity and guests of other Christian faiths, Pope John Paul II gave the following brief address.

Dear brothers and sisters,

St. Paul asks: ''Who will separate us from the love of Christ?''

As long as we remain what we are this morning—a community of prayer united in Christ, an ecclesial community of praise and worship of the Father—we shall understand and experience the answer: that no one—nothing at all—will ever separate us from the love of Christ. For us today, the Church's morning prayer is a joyful, communal celebration of God's love in Christ.

The value of the Liturgy of the Hours is enormous. Through it, all the faithful, but especially the clergy and religious, fulfill a role of prime importance: Christ's prayer goes on in the world. The Holy Spirit Himself intercedes for God's people (cf. Rom. 8:27). The Christian community, with praise and thanksgiving, glorifies the wisdom, the power, the Providence and the salvation of our God.

In this prayer of praise we lift up our hearts to the Father of our Lord Jesus Christ, bringing with us the anguish and hopes, the joys and sorrows of all our brothers and sisters in the world.

And our prayer becomes likewise a school of sensitivity, making us aware of how much our destinies are linked together in the human family. Our prayer becomes a school of love—a special kind of Christian consecrated love, by which we love the world, but with the heart of Christ.

Through this prayer of Christ to which we give voice, our day is sanctified, our activities transformed, our actions are made holy. We pray the same psalms that Jesus prayed, and come into personal contact with Him—the person to whom all Scripture points, the goal to which all history is directed.

In our celebration of the word of God, the mystery of Christ opens up before us and envelops us. And through union with our head, Jesus Christ, we become ever more increasingly one with all the members of His body. As never before, it becomes possible for us to reach out and embrace the world, but to embrace it with Christ: with authentic generosity, with pure and effective love, in service, in healing and in reconciliation.

The efficacy of our prayer renders special honor to the Father because it is made always through Christ, and for the glory of His name: "We ask this through our Lord Jesus Christ, your Son, who lives and reigns with you and the Holy Spirit, one God, for ever and ever."

As a community of prayer and praise, with the Liturgy of the Hours among the highest priorities of our day—each day—we can be sure that nothing will separate us from the love of God that is in Christ Jesus our Lord.

THE CHURCH WANTS TO COMMUNICATE CHRIST TO YOU

To some 20,000 students of Catholic Schools from New York gathered in Madison Square Garden on October 3, Pope John Paul II delivered the following discourse.

Dear young people,

I am happy to be with you in Madison Square Garden. Today this is a garden of life, where young people are alive: alive with hope and love, alive with the life of Christ. And it is in the name of Christ that I greet each one of you today.

I have been told that most of you come from the Catholic high schools. For this reason I would like to say something about Catholic education, to tell you why the Church considers it so important and expends so much energy in order to provide you and millions of other young people with a Catholic education. The answer can be summarized in one word, in one person, Jesus Christ. The Church wants to communicate Christ to you.

This is what education is all about, this is the meaning of life: to know Christ. To know Christ as a friend: as someone who cares about you and the person next to you, and all the people here and everywhere—no matter what language they speak, or what clothes they wear, or what color their skin is.

And so the purpose of Catholic education is to communicate Christ to you, so that your attitude to-

ward others will be that of Christ. You are approaching that stage in your life when you must take personal responsibility for your own destiny. Soon you will be making major decisions which will affect the whole course of your life. If these decisions reflect Christ's attitude, then your education will be a success.

We have to learn to meet challenges and even crises in the light of Christ's cross and resurrection. Part of our Catholic education is to learn to see the needs of others, to have the courage to practice what we believe in. With the support of a Catholic education we try to meet every circumstance of life with the attitude of Christ. Yes, the Church wants to communicate Christ to you so that you will come to full maturity in Him who is the perfect human being, and at the same time the Son of God.

Dear young people: you and I and all of us together make up the Church, and we are convinced that only in Christ do we find real love, and the fullness of life.

And so I invite you today to look to Christ.

When you wonder about the mystery of yourself, look to Christ who gives you the meaning of life.

When you wonder what it means to be a mature person, look to Christ who is the fullness of humanity.

And when you wonder about your role in the future of the world and of the United States, look to Christ. Only in Christ will you fulfill your potential as an American citizen and as a citizen of the world community.

With the aid of your Catholic education, you have received the greatest of gifts: the knowledge of

Christ. Of this gift St. Paul wrote: "I believe nothing can happen that will outweigh the supreme advantage of knowing Christ Jesus my Lord. For him I have accepted the loss of everything and I look on everything as so much rubbish if only I can have Christ and be given a place in him" (Phil. 3:8-9).

Be always grateful to God for this gift of knowing Christ. Be grateful also to your parents and to the community of the Church for making possible, through many sacrifices, your Catholic education. People have placed a lot of hope in you, and they now look forward to your collaboration in giving witness to Christ, and in transmitting the Gospel to others. The Church needs you. The world needs you, because it needs Christ, and you belong to Christ. And so I ask you to accept your responsibility in the Church, the responsibility of your Catholic education: to help—by your words, and, above all, by the example of your lives—to spread the Gospel. You do this by praying, and by being just and truthful and pure.

Dear young people: by a real Christian life, by the practice of your religion you are called to give witness to your faith. And because actions speak louder than words, you are called to proclaim, by the conduct of your daily lives, that you really do believe that Jesus Christ is Lord!

THE IDEAL OF LIBERTY, A MOVING FORCE

In spite of rain and bad weather, the people of New York, 300,000 strong, gathered in Battery Park on Manhattan Island, on October 3, to hear the Pope. After a brief greeting by Cardinal Cooke, the Holy Father delivered the following discourse.

Dear friends of New York,

1. My visit to your city would not have been complete without coming to Battery Park, without seeing Ellis Island and the Statue of Liberty in the distance. Every nation has its historical symbols. They may be shrines or statues or documents; but their significance lies in the truths they represent to the citizens of a nation and in the image they convey to other nations. Such a symbol in the United States is the Statue of Liberty. This is an impressive symbol of what the United States has stood for from the very beginning of its history; this is a symbol of freedom. It reflects the immigrant history of the United States, for it was freedom that millions of human beings were looking for on these shores. And it was freedom that the young Republic offered in compassion. On this spot, I wish to pay homage to this noble trait of America and its people: its desire to be free, its determination to preserve freedom, and its willingness to share this freedom with others. May the ideal of liberty, of freedom remain a moving force for your nation and for all the nations in the world today!

2. It greatly honors your country and its citizens that on this foundation of liberty you have built a na-

tion where the dignity of every human person is to be respected, where duty and honest work are held in high esteem, where generosity and hospitality are no idle words, and where the right to religious liberty is deeply rooted in your history.

Yesterday, before the General Assembly of the United Nations, I made a plea for peace and justice based on the full respect of all the fundamental rights of the human person. I also spoke of religious freedom because it regards a person's relationship to God, and because it is related in a special way to other human rights. It is closely allied with the right to freedom of conscience. If conscience is not secure in society, then the security of all other rights is threatened.

Liberty, in all its aspects, must be based on truth. I want to repeat here the words of Jesus "the truth will make you free" (Jn. 8:32). It is then my wish that your sense of freedom may always go hand in hand with a profound sense of truth and honesty about yourselves and about the realities of your society. Past achievements can never be an acceptable substitute for present responsibilities toward the common good of the society you live in and towards your fellow-citizens. Just as the desire for freedom is a universal aspiration in the world today, so is the quest for justice. No institution or organization can credibly stand for freedom today if it does not also support the quest for justice, for both are essential demands of the human spirit.

3. It will always remain one of the glorious achievements of this nation that, when people looked toward America, they received together with freedom also a chance for their own advancement. This tradition must be honored also today. The freedom that

was gained must be ratified each day by the firm rejection of whatever wounds, weakens or dishonors human life. And so I appeal to all who love freedom and justice to give a chance to all in need, to the poor and the powerless. Break open the hopeless cycles of poverty and ignorance that are still the lot of too many of our brothers and sisters; the hopeless cycles of prejudices that linger on despite enormous progress toward effective equality in education and employment; the cycles of despair in which are imprisoned all those that lack decent food, shelter or employment; the cycles of underdevelopment that are the consequence of international mechanisms that subordinate the human existence to the domination of partially conceived economic progress; and finally the inhuman cycles of war that spring from the violation of man's fundamental rights and produce still graver violation of them.

Freedom in justice will bring a new dawn of hope for the present generation as it has done before: for the homeless, for the unemployed, for the aging, for the sick and the handicapped, for the migrants and the undocumented workers, for all who hunger for human dignity in this land and in the world.

4. With sentiments of admiration and with confidence in your potential for true human greatness, I wish to greet in you the rich variety of your nation, where people of different ethnic origins and creeds can live, work and prosper together in freedom and mutual respect. I greet and I thank for the cordial welcome of all those who joined me here, businessmen and laborers, scholars and managers, social workers and civil servants, old and young, I greet you with respect, esteem and love. My warm greetings go to each

and every group, to my fellow Catholics, to the members of the different Christian Churches with whom I am united in the faith in Jesus Christ.

And I address a special word of greeting to the leaders of the Jewish community whose presence here honors me greatly. A few months ago, I met with an international group of Jewish representatives in Rome. On that occasion, recalling the initiatives undertaken following the Second Vatican Council under my predecessor Paul VI, I stated that "our two communities are connected and closely related at the very level of their respective religious identities," and that on this basis "we recognize with utmost clarity that the path along which we should proceed is one of fraternal dialogue and fruitful collaboration" (*L'Osservatore Romano,* March 12-13, 1979). I am glad to ascertain that this same path has been followed here, in the United States, by large sections of both communities and their respective authorities and representative bodies. Several common programs of study, mutual knowledge, a common determination to reject all forms of anti-semitism and discrimination, and various forms of collaboration for the human advancement, inspired by our common biblical heritage, have created deep and permanent links between Jews and Catholics. As one who in my homeland has shared the suffering of your brethren, I greet you with the word taken from the Hebrew language: Shalom! Peace be with you.

And to everyone here I offer the expression of my respect, my esteem and my fraternal love. May God bless all of you! May God bless New York!

A CITY MUST
HAVE A SOUL!

At Shea Stadium, in the Queens quarter of New York City, Pope John Paul had his last meeting with the people of the city. The Pope's entry into the stadium was greeted with joyful exclamations, not only in English but also in Polish and Italian, in which languages the Holy Father also responded.

The following is the discourse of the Pope.

Dear friends in New York,

It gives me great joy to have the opportunity to come and greet you on my way to La Guardia Airport, at the end of my visit to the Archdiocese and to the metropolis of New York.

Thank you for your warm welcome. In you I wish to greet once again all the people of New York, Long Island, New Jersey and Connecticut, Brooklyn: all your parishes, hospitals, schools and organizations, your sick and aged. And with special affection I greet the young people and the children.

From Rome I bring you a message of faith and love. "May the peace of Christ reign in your hearts!" (Col. 3:15) Make peace the desire of your heart, for if you love peace, you will love all humanity, without distinction of race, color or creed.

My greeting is also an invitation to all of you to feel personally responsible for the well-being and the community spirit of your city. A visitor to New York is always impressed by the special character of this metropolis: skyscrapers, endless streets, large residential areas, housing blocks, and above all the millions of people who live here or who look here for the work that will sustain them and their family.

Large concentrations of people create special problems and special needs. The personal effort and loyal collaboration of everybody are needed to find the right solutions, so that all men, women and children can live in dignity and develop to the full their potential without having to suffer for lack of education, housing, employment, and cultural opportunities. Above all, a city needs a soul if it is to become a true home for human beings. You, the people, must give it this soul. And how do you do this? By loving each other. Love for each other must be the hallmark of your lives. In the Gospel Jesus Christ tells us: "You shall love your neighbor as yourself" (Mt. 22:39). This commandment of the Lord must be your inspiration in forming true human relationships among yourselves, so that nobody will ever feel alone or unwanted, or much less, rejected, despised or hated. Jesus Himself will give you the power of fraternal love. And every neighborhood, every block, every street will become a true community because you will want it so, and Jesus will help you to bring it about.

Keep Jesus Christ in your hearts, and you will recognize His face in every human being. You will want to help Him out in all His needs: the needs of your brothers and sisters. This is the way we prepare ourselves to meet Jesus, when He will come again, on the last day, as the Judge of the living and the dead and He will say to us: "Come, you have my Father's blessing! Inherit the kingdom prepared for you from the creation of the world. For I was hungry and you gave me food, I was thirsty and you gave me drink. I was a stranger and you welcomed me, naked and you

clothed me. I was ill and you comforted me, in prison and you came to visit me... I assure you as often as you did it for one of my least brethren, you did it for ME" (Mt. 25:34-35, 39).

The Holy Father then continued in Spanish.

I now wish to address a very cordial welcome to each and every member of the Spanish-speaking colony, coming from various countries, here in this Stadium.

In you, I see and I wish to greet, with great affection, the whole of the numerous Hispanic community living in New York and many other places in the United States.

I wish to assure you that I am well aware of the place that you occupy in American society, and that I follow with lively interest your accomplishments, aspirations and difficulties within the social fabric of this nation, which is your homeland of adoption or the land that welcomes you. For this reason, from the very moment that I accepted the invitation to visit this country, I thought of you, who are integral and a specific part of this society, a very considerable part of the Church in this vast nation.

I wish to exhort you, as Catholics, always to maintain very clearly your Christian identity, with a constant reference to the value of your faith, values that must enlighten the legitimate quest for a worthy material position for yourselves and your families.

Since you are generally immersed in the environment of heavily populated cities and in a social climate where sometimes technology and material values take first place, make an effort to provide a spiritual contribution to your life and your neighborhood. Keep close to God in your lives, to the God who calls you to be ever more worthy of your condition as human beings with an eternal vocation, to the God who invites you to solidarity and to collaboration in building up an ever more human, just and fraternal world.

I pray for you, for your families and friends, above all for your children, for the sick and suffering, and to all of you I give my blessing. May God be with you always!

Finally he concluded in English with the words:

Good-bye, and God bless you.

REMEMBERING
ST. JOHN NEUMANN

*On October 3, during a brief ceremony at the Philadelphia air-
port, His Holiness was welcomed by Cardinal Krol, his auxili-
aries, the Governor of Pennsylvania, the Mayor of Philadelphia,
and hundreds of people. He then went to the Cathedral, where
after a short address by Cardinal Krol, he delivered the following
discourse.*

Dear brothers and sisters in Christ,

I give thanks to the Lord for permitting me to
come back to this city of Philadelphia, to this state of
Pennsylvania. I have very happy memories of being
here before as your guest, and I remember especially
the bicentennial celebration in 1976 that I attended as
Archbishop of Krakow. Today, by the grace of God, I
come here as successor of Peter to bring you a message of love and to strengthen you in your faith. In
your kind welcome I feel that you want to honor in
me the Christ whom I represent and who lives in all
of us—all of us who through the Holy Spirit form one
community, one communion in faith and love. I feel
moreover that I am truly among friends, and I feel
very much at home in your midst.

In a very particular way I wish to thank you, Cardinal Krol, Archbishop of Philadelphia, for the invitation you extended to me, to come here and celebrate
the Eucharist together with you and your people. A
heartfelt greeting also goes to the clergy, religious and
laity, of this local church. I have come as your brother
in Christ, bringing with me the same message that the
Lord Jesus Himself brought to the villages and cities

in the Holy Land: let us praise the Lord our God and Father, and let us love one another!

It gives me great pleasure to meet you here in the Cathedral of Philadelphia, for it has a deep meaning for me. Above all, it means *you:* the living Church of Christ, here and now, alive in faith, united in the love of Jesus Christ.

This Cathedral recalls the memory of St. John Neumann, once Bishop of this See, and now and forever a saint of the universal Church. In this edifice, his message and his example of holiness must continually be transmitted to every new generation of young people. And if we listen carefully today we can hear St. John Neumann speaking to all of us in the words of the letter to the Hebrews: "Remember your leaders who spoke the word of God to you; consider how their lives ended, and imitate their faith. Jesus Christ is the same yesterday, today and forever" (Heb. 13:8).

Finally, this Cathedral links you to the great Apostles of Rome, Peter and Paul. They, in turn, continue to give you their testimony to Christ, to proclaim to you Christ's divinity, to acknowledge Him before the world. Here today in Philadelphia, the confession of Peter becomes for all of us a personal act of faith, and this act of faith we make together, as we say to Jesus: "You are the Christ, the Son of the living God" (Mt. 16:16). And with St. Paul, each one of us is called to say in the depths of our hearts and before the world: "I still live my human life, but it is a life of faith in the Son of God, who loved me and gave himself for me" (Gal. 2:20).

This Cathedral is also linked in religion to the heritage of this historic city. Every service to morality and spirituality is a service to the civilization of man; it is a contribution to human happiness and to true well-being.

And so, from this Cathedral I offer my greetings to the whole city of Philadelphia, the civil authorities and all the people. As the city of brotherly love, as the first capital of the United States of America, you are a symbol of freedom and fraternal relations. My greeting is also a prayer. May the common dedication and the united efforts of all your citizens—Catholics, Protestants and Jews alike—succeed in making your inner city and suburbs places where people are no strangers to each other, where every man, woman and child feels respected; where nobody feels abandoned, rejected or alone.

Asking for your prayerful support for my visit of friendship and pastoral concern, I extend my blessing to all of you, to those present here today, to your dear ones at home, to the aged and the sick, and in a very special way to all the young people and the children.

God bless Philadelphia!

STRIVE TO PRESERVE THE VALUES OF THE DECLARATION OF INDEPENDENCE

The first Eucharistic Celebration of Pope John Paul in Philadelphia took place in the afternoon of October 3, at Logan Circle where an immense crowd of people was waiting.

During the Mass the Holy Father delivered the following homily.

Dear brothers and sisters of the Church in Philadelphia,

1. It is a great joy for me to celebrate the Eucharist with you today. All of us are gathered together as one community, one people in the grace and peace of God our Father and of the Lord Jesus Christ; we are gathered in the fellowship of the Holy Spirit. We have come together to proclaim the Gospel in all its power, for the Eucharistic Sacrifice is the summit and enactment of our proclamation:

Christ has died, Christ is risen, Christ will come again! From this altar of sacrifice, there arises a hymn of praise and thanksgiving to God through Jesus Christ. We who belong to Christ are all part of this hymn, this sacrifice of praise. The sacrifice of Calvary is renewed on this altar, and it becomes our offering too—an offering for the benefit of the living and the dead, an offering for the universal Church.

Assembled in the charity of Christ, we are all one in His sacrifice: the Cardinal Archbishop who is called to lead this Church in the path of truth and love; his Auxiliary Bishops and the diocesan and religious clergy, who share with the Bishops in the preaching of the word; men and women religious, who through the consecration of their lives show the world what it means to be faithful to the message of the Beatitudes; fathers and mothers, with their great mission of building up the Church in love; every category of the laity with their particular task in the Church's mission of evangelization and salvation. This sacrifice offered today in Philadelphia is the expression of our praying community. In union with Jesus Christ we make intercession for the universal Church, for the well-being of all our fellow men and women, and today, in particular, for the preservation of all the human and Christian values that are the heritage of this land, this country and this very city.

2. Philadelphia is the city of the Declaration of Independence, that remarkable document, containing a solemn attestation of the equality of all human beings, endowed by their Creator with certain inalienable rights: life, liberty and the pursuit of happiness, expressing a "firm reliance on the protection of divine Providence." These are the sound moral principles formulated by your Founding Fathers and enshrined forever in your history. In the human and civil values that are contained in the spirit of this Declaration there are easily recognized strong connections with basic religious and Christian values. A sense of religion itself is part of this heritage. The Liberty Bell which I visited on another occasion proudly bears the words of the Bible: "Proclaim liberty throughout the

land'' (Lev. 25:10). This tradition poses for all future generations of America a noble challenge: "One Nation under God, indivisible, with liberty and justice for all.''

3. As citizens, you must strive to preserve these human values, to understand them better and to define their consequences for the whole community, and as a worthy contribution to the world. As Christians, you must strengthen these human values and complement them by confronting them with the Gospel message, so that you may discover their deeper meaning, and thus assume more fully your duties and obligations toward your fellow human beings, with whom you are bound in a common destiny. In a way, for us, who know Jesus Christ, human and Christian values are but two aspects of the same reality: the reality of man, redeemed by Christ and called to the fullness of eternal life.

In my first encyclical letter, I stated this important truth: "Christ, the Redeemer of the world, is the one who penetrated in a unique unrepeatable way into the mystery of man and entered his 'heart.' Rightly therefore does the Second Vatican Council teach: 'The truth is that only in the mystery of the Incarnate Word does the mystery of man take on light. For Adam, the first man, was a type of Him who was to come (Rom. 5:14), Christ the Lord. Christ the new Adam, in the very revelation of the mystery of the Father and His love, fully reveals man to himself and brings to light his most high calling' '' (*Redemptor hominis,* 8). It is then in Jesus Christ that every man, woman and child is called to find the answer to the questions regarding the values that will inspire his or her personal and social relations.

4. How then can a Christian, inspired and guided
by the mystery of the Incarnation and Redemption of
Christ, strengthen his or her own values and those
that are embodied in the heritage of this nation? The
answer to that question, in order to be complete,
would have to be long. Let me, however, just touch
upon a few important points. These values are
strengthened: when power and authority are exercised in full respect for all the fundamental rights of
the human person, whose dignity is the dignity of one
created in the image and likeness of God (Gen. 1:26);

when freedom is accepted, not as an absolute end in itself, but as a gift that enables self-giving and service; when the family is protected and strengthened, when its unity is preserved, and when its role as the basic cell of society is recognized and honored. Human-Christian values are fostered when every effort is made so that no child anywhere in the world faces death because of lack of food, or faces a diminished intellectual and physical potential for want of sufficient nourishment, or has to bear all through life the scars of deprivation. Human-Christian values triumph when any system is reformed that authorizes the exploitation of any human being; when upright service and honesty in public servants is promoted; when the dispensing of justice is fair and the same for all; when responsible use is made of the material and energy resources of the world—resources that are meant for the benefit of all; when the environment is preserved intact for the future generations. Human-Christian values triumph by subjecting political and economic considerations to human dignity, by making them serve the cause of man—every person created by God, every brother and sister redeemed by Christ.

5. I have mentioned the Declaration of Independence and the Liberty Bell, two monuments that exemplify the spirit of freedom on which this country was founded. Your attachment to liberty, to freedom, is part of your heritage. When the Liberty Bell rang for the first time in 1776, it was to announce the freedom of your nation, the beginning of the pursuit of a common destiny independent of any outside coercion. This principle of freedom is paramount in the political and social order, in relationships between the

government and the people, and between individual and individual. However, man's life is also lived in another order of reality: in the order of his relationship to what is objectively true and morally good. Freedom thus acquires a deeper meaning when it is referred to the human person. It concerns in the first place the relation of man to himself. Every human person, endowed with reason, is free when he is the master of his own actions, when he is capable of choosing that good which is in conformity with reason, and therefore with his own human dignity.

Freedom can never tolerate an offense against the rights of others, and one of the fundamental rights of man is the right to worship God. In the Declaration on Religious Freedom, the Second Vatican Council stated that the "demand for freedom in human society chiefly regards the quest for the values proper to the human spirit. It regards in the first place, the free exercise of religion in society.... Religious freedom, which men demand as necessary to fulfill their duty to worship God, has to do with immunity from coercion in civil society. Therefore it leaves untouched traditional Catholic teaching on the moral duty of men and societies toward the true religion and toward the one Church of Christ" (Dignitatis humanae, 1).

6. Christ Himself linked freedom with the knowledge of truth. "You will know the truth and the truth will make you free" (Jn. 8:32). In my first encyclical I wrote in this regard: "These words contain both a fundamental requirement and a warning: the requirement of an honest relationship with regard to truth as a condition for authentic freedom, and the warning to avoid every kind of illusory freedom, every super-

ficial unilateral freedom, every freedom that fails to enter into the whole truth about man and the world" (Redemptor hominis, 12).

Freedom can therefore never be construed without relation to the truth as revealed by Jesus Christ, and proposed by His Church, nor can it be seen as a pretext for moral anarchy, for every moral order must remain linked to truth. St. Peter, in his first letter, says: "Live as free men, but do not use your freedom for malice" (1 Pt. 2:16). No freedom can exist when it goes against man in what he is, or against man in his relationship to others and to God.

This is especially relevant when one considers the domain of human sexuality. Here, as in any other field, there can be no true freedom without respect for the truth regarding the nature of human sexuality and marriage. In today's society, we see so many disturbing tendencies and so much laxity regarding the Christian view on sexuality that have all one thing in common: recourse to the concept of freedom to justify any behavior that is no longer consonant with the true moral order and the teaching of the Church. Moral norms do not militate against the freedom of the person or the couple; on the contrary they exist precisely for that freedom, since they are given to ensure the right use of freedom. Whoever refuses to accept these norms and to act accordingly, whoever seeks to liberate himself or herself from these norms, is not truly free. Free indeed is the person who models his or her behavior in a responsible way according to the exigencies of the objective good. What I have said here regards the whole of conjugal morality, but it applies as well to the priests with regard to the obligations of celibacy. The cohesion of freedom and ethics has also its consequences for the pursuit of the common good in society and for the national independence which the Liberty Bell announced two centuries ago.

7. Divine law is the sole standard of human liberty and is given to us in the Gospel of Christ, the Gospel of Redemption. But fidelity to this Gospel of Redemption will never be possible without the action of the Holy Spirit. It is the Holy Spirit who guards the life-giving message entrusted to the Church. It is the Holy Spirit who ensures the faithful transmission of the Gospel into the lives of all of us. It is by the action of the Holy Spirit that the Church is built up day after day into a kingdom: a kingdom of truth and life, a kingdom of holiness and grace, a universal kingdom of justice, love and peace.

Today, therefore, we come before the Father to offer Him the petitions and desires of our hearts, to offer Him praise and thanksgiving. We do this from the city of Philadelphia for the universal Church and for the world. We do this as "members of the household of God" (Eph. 2:19) in union with the sacrifice of Christ Jesus, our cornerstone, for the glory of the most Holy Trinity. Amen.

GREAT PROMISE FOR THE FUTURE OF EVANGELIZATION

After the Mass in Logan Circle the Holy Father later went to St. Charles Seminary to meet the priests, religious and seminarians of the archdiocese. He spoke to them as follows:

Beloved brothers and sons in Christ,

One of the things I wanted most to do during my visit to the United States has now arrived. I wanted to visit a seminary and meet the seminarians; and through you I would like to communicate to all seminarians how much you mean to me, and how much you mean for the future of the Church—for the future of the mission given to us by Christ.

You hold a special place in my thoughts and prayers. In your lives there is great promise for the future of evangelization. And you give us hope that the authentic renewal of the Church which was begun by the Second Vatican Council will be brought to fruition. But in order for this to happen, you must receive a solid and well-rounded preparation in the seminary. This personal conviction about the importance of seminaries prompted me to write these words in my Holy Thursday Letter to the Bishops of the Church: "The full reconstitution of the life of the seminaries throughout the Church will be the best proof of the achievement of the renewal to which the Council directed the Church."

1. If seminaries are to fulfill their mission in the Church two activities in the overall program of the seminary are crucially important: the teaching of God's Word, and discipline.

The intellectual formation of the priest, which is so vital for the times in which we live, embraces a number of the human sciences as well as the various sacred sciences. These all have an important place in your preparation for the priesthood. But the first priority for seminaries today is the teaching of God's Word in all its purity and integrity, with all its demands and in all its power. This was clearly affirmed by my beloved predecessor Paul VI, when he stated that Sacred Scripture is "a perpetual source of spiritual life, the chief instrument for handing down Christian doctrine, and the center of all theological study" (Apostolic Constitution *Missale romanum,* April 3, 1969). Therefore if you, the seminarians of this generation, are to be adequately prepared to take on the heritage and challenge of the Second Vatican Council you will need to be well trained in the Word of God.

Secondly, the seminary must provide a sound discipline to prepare for a life of consecrated service in the image of Christ. Its purpose was well defined by the Second Vatican Council: "The discipline required by seminary life should not be regarded merely as a strong support of community life and of charity. For it is a necessary part of the whole training program designed to provide self-mastery, to foster solid maturity of personality, and to develop other traits of character which are extremely serviceable for the ordered and productive activity of the Church" *(Optatam totius,* 11).

When discipline is properly exercised, it can create an atmosphere of recollection which enables the seminarian to develop interiorly those attitudes which are so desirable in a priest, such as joyful obedience, generosity and self-sacrifice. In the different forms of community life that are appropriate for the seminary, you will learn the art of dialogue: the capacity to listen to others and to discover the richness of their personality, and the ability to give of yourself. Seminary discipline will reinforce, rather than diminish your freedom, for it will help develop in you those traits and attitudes of mind and heart which God has given you, and which enrich your humanity and help you to serve more effectively His people. Discipline will also assist you in ratifying day after day in your hearts the obedience you owe to Christ and His Church.

2. I want to remind you of the importance of fidelity. Before you can be ordained, you are called by Christ to make a free and irrevocable commitment to be faithful to Him and to His Church. Human dignity requires that you maintain this commitment, that you keep your promise to Christ no matter what difficulties you may encounter, and no matter what temptations you may be exposed to. The seriousness of this irrevocable commitment places a special obligation upon the rector and faculty of the seminary—and in a particular way on the spiritual director—to help you to evaluate your own suitability for Ordination. It is then the responsibility of the Bishop to judge whether you should be called to the priesthood.

It is important that one's commitment be made with full awareness and personal freedom. And so during these years in the seminary, take time to reflect on the serious obligations and the difficulties which are part of the priest's life. Consider whether Christ is calling you to the celibate life. You can make a responsible decision for celibacy only after you have reached the firm conviction that Christ is indeed offering you this gift, which is intended for the good of the Church and for the service of others (cf. Letter to Priests, 9).

To understand what it means to be faithful we must look to Christ, the "faithful witness" (Rev. 1:5), the Son who "learned to obey through what he suffered" (Heb. 5:8); to Jesus who said: "My aim is to do not my own will, but the will of him who sent me" (Jn. 5:30). We look to Jesus, not only to see and contemplate His fidelity to the Father despite all opposition (cf. Heb. 12:3), but also to learn from Him the means He employed in order to be faithful: especially prayer and abandonment to God's will (cf. Lk. 22:39ff.).

Remember that in the final analysis perseverance in fidelity is a proof, not of human strength and courage, but of the efficacy of Christ's grace. And so if we are going to persevere we shall have to be men of prayer who, through the Eucharist, the Liturgy of the Hours and our personal encounters with Christ, find the courage and grace to be faithful. Let us be confident then, remembering the words of St. Paul: "There is nothing that I cannot master with the help of the one who gives me strength" (Phil. 4:13).

3. My brothers and sons in Christ, keep in mind the priorities of the priesthood to which you aspire: namely, prayer and the ministry of the Word (Acts 6:4).

"It is the prayer that shows the essential style of the priest; without prayer this style becomes deformed. Prayer helps us always to find the light that has led us since the beginning of our priestly vocation, and which never ceases to lead us.... Prayer enables us to be converted continually, to remain in a state of continuous reaching out to God, which is essential if we wish to lead others to Him. Prayer helps us to believe, to hope and to love..." (Letter to Priests, 10).

It is my hope that during your years in the seminary you will develop an ever greater hunger for the Word of God (cf. Amos 8:11). Meditate on this Word daily and study it continually, so that your whole life may become a proclamation of Christ, the Word made flesh (cf. Jn. 1:14). In this Word of God are the beginning and end of all ministry, the purpose of all pastoral activity, the rejuvenating source for faithful perseverance and the one thing which can give meaning and unity to the varied activities of a priest.

4. "Let the message of Christ, in all its richness, find a home with you" (Col. 3:16). In the knowledge of Christ you have the key to the Gospel. In the knowledge of Christ you have an understanding of the needs of the world. Since He became one with us in all things but sin, your union with Jesus of Nazareth could never, and will never be an obstacle to understanding and responding to the needs of the world. And finally, in the knowledge of Christ, you will not only discover and come to understand the limitations of human wisdom and of human solutions to the needs of humanity, but you will also experience the power of Jesus, and the value of human reason

and human endeavor when they are taken up in the strength of Jesus, when they are redeemed in Christ.

May our Blessed Mother Mary protect you today and always.

5. May I also take this opportunity to greet the lay people who are present today at St. Charles Seminary. Your presence here is a sign of your esteem for the ministerial priesthood, as well as being a reminder of that close cooperation between laity and priests which is needed if the mission of Christ is to be fulfilled in our time. I am happy that you are present and I am grateful for all that you do for the Church in Philadelphia. In particular I ask you to pray for these young men, and for all seminarians that they may persevere in their calling. Please pray for all priests and for the success of their ministry among God's people. And please pray the Lord of the harvest to send more laborers into His vineyard, the Church.

THE LESSON TO LEARN FROM THE LIFE OF ST. JOHN NEUMANN

On October 4, the Holy Father made a brief visit to the tomb of St. John Neumann, the great apostle of immigrants who was canonized a few years ago. To the faithful who had gathered in St. Peter's Church, the Holy Father spoke as follows:

Dear brothers and sisters in Christ,

I have come to St. Peter's Church to pray at the tomb of St. John Neumann, a zealous missionary, a dedicated pastor, a faithful son of St. Alphonsus in the Congregation of the Most Holy Redeemer, and the fourth Bishop of Philadelphia.

As I stand in this church, I am reminded of the one thing which motivated St. John Neumann throughout his life: his love for Christ. His own prayers show us this love; for from the time he was a child he used to say: "Jesus, for You I want to live; for You I want to die; I want to be all Yours in life; I want to be all Yours in death" (Nicola Ferrante, *S. Giovanni Neumann, CSSR, Pioniere del Vangelo,* p. 25). And at the First Mass he celebrated as a priest, he prayed in these words: "Lord, give me holiness."

My brothers and sisters in Christ: this is the lesson we learn from the life of St. John Neumann, and the message which I leave with you today: what really matters in life is that we are loved by Christ, and that we love Him in return. In comparison to the love of Jesus, everything else is secondary. And without the love of Jesus, everything else is useless.

May Mary, our Mother of Perpetual Help, intercede for us; may St. John Neumann pray for us; and with the help of their prayers may we persevere in faith, be joyful in hope and be strengthened in our love for Jesus Christ, our Redeemer and our Lord.

MEMBERS OF THE UNIVERSAL CHURCH AND CITIZENS OF THIS WORLD

During the lifetime of St. John Neumann the parishioners of St. Peter's were mostly of German origin. Since that time the parish has seen substantial changes in the composition of its members. To the many Spanish-speaking people who are now in the parish, the Holy Father, after his discourse in English, spoke in Spanish as follows:

Beloved Spanish-speaking brothers and sisters,

I greet you with joy and I am grateful for your enthusiastic presence here, in St. Peter's Church, where there rest the remains of St. John Neumann, the first American man to be canonized.

You have gathered in this place in large numbers, members of the Spanish-speaking community, who arrived in this country as emigrants or who were born here of emigrant families, but who preserve the Christian faith as the principal treasure of your tradition.

St. John Neumann, too, was an emigrant and knew many of the difficulties that you have met with: that of language, a different culture, and social adaptation.

Your effort and perseverance in preserving your own religious heritage is well known. At the same time, however, it is put in the service of the whole national community, in order that it may be a testimony of unity within a pluralism of religion, culture and social life.

Being faithful to the saving message of Jesus Christ, your ecclesial communities will find the right way to feel they are members of the universal Church and citizens of this world.

May devotion to Mary, our Mother, and your communion with the Vicar of Christ, continue to be always, as up to now, the power that nourishes and increases your Christian faith.

I most willingly give a special apostolic blessing to all of you present here, to all those who have not been able to come, in particular the sick and the old, who are spiritually associated with this meeting.

THE ROLE OF THE UKRAINIAN TRADITION IN THE CATHOLIC CHURCH

On October 4, after visiting the tomb of St. John Neumann, the Holy Father then met the Ukrainian community in their cathedral dedicated to the Immaculate Conception. After an address of homage in both Ukrainian and English by the Archbishop of Philadelphia of the Ukrainians, Most Rev. Myroslav Lubachivsky, the Pope replied as follows, beginning in Ukrainian and continuing in English.

Praised be Jesus Christ!

With this Christian greeting I address you, dear brothers and sisters, in your native Ukrainian language before beginning to speak to you in English.

In the first place I greet all the members of the Hierarchy here present, both of the metropolitan area of Philadelphia, as well as that of Pittsburgh.

I greet all the dear priests and religious men and women.

I cordially salute all you, dear faithful of the Ukrainian metropolitan area of Philadelphia, who are gathered here in this temple of the Most Holy Mother of God, to honor in my person the successor of St. Peter in the See of Rome, the Vicar of Christ on earth.

On all of you, dear brothers and sisters, I invoke copious graces from almighty God, through the intercession of the Immaculate Virgin Mary, to whom your cathedral is dedicated.

I bless you all from the bottom of my heart. Praised be Jesus Christ!

The Pope then continued in English.

Dear brothers and sisters,

"Now in Christ Jesus...you are citizens like all the saints, and part of God's household. You are of a building that has the apostles and prophets for its foundations, and Christ Jesus Himself for its main cornerstone" (Eph. 2:13, 19-20). With these words the Apostle Paul reminded the Ephesians of the tremendous blessing they had received in becoming members of the Church. And those words are still true today. You are part of the household of God. You, members of Ukrainian tradition, are part of a building that has the apostles and prophets for its foundations, and Christ Jesus Himself for its main cornerstone. This has all occurred according to the providential plan of God.

Several years ago, my beloved predecessor, Paul VI, gave a stone from the tomb of St. Peter to be included in the construction of this beautiful cathedral dedicated to Mary Immaculate. Pope Paul intended this gift to be a visible symbol of the love and esteem of the Apostolic See of Rome for the Ukrainian Church. At the same time, this stone was meant to serve as a sign of the fidelity of the Ukrainian Church to the See of Peter. In this profound symbolic gesture, Paul VI was reaffirming the teaching of the Apostle Paul in the letter to the Ephesians.

Today, as successor to Paul VI in the Chair of St. Peter, I come to visit you in this magnificent new cathedral. I am happy for this opportunity. I welcome the occasion to assure you, as universal pastor of the

Church, that all who have inherited the Ukrainian tradition have an important and distinguished part to fulfill in the Catholic Church.

As history testifies, the Church developed a number of rites and traditions as in the course of time she spread from Jerusalem to the nations and took flesh in the language, culture and human traditions of the individual peoples who accepted the Gospel with open hearts. These various rites and traditions, far from being a sign of deviation, infidelity or disunity, were in fact unfailing proof of the presence of the Holy Spirit who continually renews and enriches the Church, the kingdom of Christ already present in mystery (cf. *Lumen gentium,* 3).

The various traditions within the Church give expression to the multitude of ways the Gospel can take root and flower in the lives of God's people. They are living evidence of the richness of the Church. Each one, while united to all the others in the "same faith, the same sacraments and the same government" (Orientalium ecclesiarum, 2), is nevertheless manifested in its own liturgy, ecclesiastical discipline and spiritual patrimony. Each tradition combined particular artistic expressions and unique spiritual insights with an unparalleled lived experience of being faithful to Christ. It was in view of these considerations that the Second Vatican Council declared: "History, tradition, and numerous ecclesiastical institutions clearly manifest how much the universal Church is indebted to the Eastern Churches. Thus this sacred Synod not only honors this ecclesiastical and spiritual heritage with merited esteem and rightful praise, but also unhesitatingly looks upon it as the heritage of Christ's universal Church" (Orientalium ecclesiarum, 5).

For many years, I have highly esteemed the Ukrainian people. I have known of the many sufferings and injustices you have endured. These have been and continue to be matters of great concern to me. I am also mindful of the struggles of the Ukrainian Catholic Church, throughout its history, to remain faithful to the Gospel and to be in union with the successor of St. Peter. I cannot forget the countless Ukrainian martyrs, in ancient and more recent times, most of whose names are unknown, who gave up their lives rather than abandon their faith. I mention these in order to show my profound esteem for the Ukrainian Church and its proved fidelity in suffering.

I also wish to mention those things which you have preserved as your special spiritual patrimony: the Slavonic liturgical language, the ecclesiastical music and the numerous forms of piety which have developed over the centuries and continue to nourish your lives. Your appreciation of these treasures of the Ukrainian tradition is demonstrated by the way that you have maintained your attachment with the Ukrainian Church and have continued to live the faith according to its unique tradition.

My brothers and sisters in Christ, I want to recall in your presence the words Jesus prayed on the vigil of His death upon the cross: "Father...that they may be one" (Jn. 17:11). We must never forget this prayer; in fact we must continually search for still better ways to safeguard and strengthen the bonds of union which unite us in the one Catholic Church.

Remember the words of St. Paul: "You form part of a building that has the apostles and prophets for its foundations, and Christ Jesus himself for its main cornerstone" (Eph. 2:20). The unity of this spiritual building, which is the Church, is preserved by fidelity to the cornerstone, who is Christ, and to the teaching of the apostles preserved and explained in the Tradition of the Church. A real unity of doctrine binds us as one.

Catholic unity also entails a recognition of the successor of St. Peter and his ministry of strengthening and preserving intact the communion of the universal Church, while safeguarding the existence of legitimate individual traditions within it. The Ukrainian Church, as well as the other Eastern Churches, has a right and duty, in accordance with the teaching of the Council (cf. *Orientalium ecclesiarum,* 5), to preserve its own ecclesiastical and spiritual patrimony. It is precisely because these individual traditions are also intended for the enrichment of the universal Church that the Apostolic See of Rome takes great care to protect and foster each one. In turn, the ecclesial communities that follow these traditions are called to adhere with love and respect to certain particular forms of discipline which my predecessors and I, in fulfilling our pastoral responsibility to the universal Church, have judged necessary for the well-being of the whole body of Christ.

To a great extent, our Catholic unity depends on mutual charity. Let us remember that the unity of the Church originated on the cross of Christ, which broke down the barriers of sin and division and reconciled us with God and with one another. Jesus foretold this unifying act when He said: "...and I, if I be lifted up from the earth, will draw all men to myself" (Jn. 12:32). If we continue to imitate the love of Jesus, our Savior, on the cross, and if we persevere in love for one another, then we shall preserve the bonds of unity in the Church and witness the fulfillment of Jesus' prayer: "Father...that they may be one" (Jn. 17:11).

As for the future, I entrust you to the protection of Mary Immaculate, the Mother of God, the Mother of the Church. I know that you honor her with great devotion. This magnificent cathedral dedicated to the Immaculate Conception bears eloquent witness to your filial love. And for centuries, our Blessed Mother has been the strength of your people throughout their sufferings, and her loving intercession has been a cause of their joy.

Continue to entrust yourselves to her protection.

Continue to be faithful to her Son, our Lord Jesus Christ, the Redeemer of the world.

And may the grace of our Lord Jesus Christ be with you all.

SACRAMENTAL PRIESTHOOD IS TRULY A GIFT FROM GOD

The last encounter of Pope John Paul in the city of Philadelphia was the solemn concelebration on October 4 with representatives of the councils of priests of all the dioceses in the United States. Held in the Civic Center of the metropolis, the meeting included hundreds of religious men and women, as well as seminarians.

After the Gospel, the Holy Father delivered the following homily.

Dear brother priests,

1. As we celebrate this Mass, which brings together the presidents or chairmen of the priests' senates, or councils, of all the dioceses of the United States, the theme that suggests itself to our reflection is a vital one: the priesthood itself and its central importance to the task of the Church. In the Encyclical Letter *Redemptor hominis,* I described this task in these words: "The Church's fundamental function in every age and particularly in ours is to direct man's gaze, to point the awareness and experience of the whole of humanity towards the mystery of God, to help men to be familiar with the profundity of the Redemption taking place in Christ Jesus" *(Redemptor hominis,* 10).

SIGN OF UNITY

Priests' senates are a new structure in the Church, called for by the Second Vatican Council and recent Church legislation. This new structure gives a concrete expression to the unity of Bishop and priests in the service of shepherding the flock of Christ, and it assists the Bishop in his distinctive role of governing the diocese, by guaranteeing for him the counsel of representative advisers from among the presbyterium. Our concelebration of today's Eucharist is intended to be a mark of affirmation for the good that has been achieved by your priests' senates during these past years, as well as an encouragement to pursue with enthusiasm and determination this important aim, which is "to bring the life and activity of the People of God into greater conformity with the Gospel" (cf. *Ecclesiae sanctae*, 16:1). Most of all, however, I want this Mass to be the special occasion on which I can speak through you to all my brother priests throughout this nation about our priesthood. With great love I repeat the words that I wrote to you on Holy Thursday: "For you I am a Bishop, with you I am a priest."

GOD GIVES VOCATIONS

Our priestly vocation is given by the Lord Jesus Himself. It is a call which is personal and individual: we are called by name as was Jeremiah. It is a call to service: we are sent out to preach the Good News, to "give God's flock a shepherd's care." It is a call to communion of purpose and of action: to be one priesthood with Jesus and with one another, just as Jesus and His Father are one—a unity so beautifully symbolized in this concelebrated Mass.

Priesthood is not merely a task which has been assigned; it is a vocation, a call to be heard again and again. To hear this call and to respond generously to

what this call entails is a task for each priest, but it is also a responsibility for the senates of priests. This responsibility means deepening our understanding of the priesthood as Christ instituted it, as He wanted it to be and to remain, and as the Church faithfully explains it and transmits it. Fidelity to the call to the priesthood means building up this priesthood with God's people by a life of service according to apostolic priorities: concentration "on prayer and the ministry of the word" (Acts 6:4).

In the Gospel of St. Mark the priestly call of the twelve apostles is like a bud whose flowering displays a whole theology of priesthood. In the midst of Jesus' ministry, we read that "he went up the mountain and summoned the men he himself had decided on, who came and joined him. He named twelve as his companions whom he would send to preach the good news...." The passage then lists the names of the twelve (Mk. 3:13-14). Here we see three significant aspects of the call given by Jesus: He called His first priests individually and by *name;* He called them for the service of His Word, *to preach the Gospel;* and He made them His own *companions,* drawing them into that unity of life and action which He shares with His Father in the very life of the Trinity.

PROPHETIC CALL

2. Let us explore these three dimensions of our priesthood by reflecting on today's Scripture readings. For it is in the tradition of the prophetic call that the Gospel places the priestly vocation of the twelve apostles by Jesus. When the priest reflects on Jeremiah's call to be a prophet, he is both reassured and

disturbed. "Have no fear...because I am with you to deliver you," says the Lord to the one whom He calls.... "For look, I place *my* words in your mouth." Who would not take heart at hearing such divine assurance? Yet when we consider *why* such reassurance is needed, do we not see in ourselves that same reluctance we find in Jeremiah's reply? Like him, at times, our concept of this ministry is too earth-bound; we lack confidence in Him who calls us. We can also become too attached to our own vision of ministry, thinking that it depends too much on our own talents and abilities, and at times forgetting that it is God who calls us, as He called Jeremiah from the womb. Nor is it our work or our ability that is primary: we are called to speak the words of God and not our own; to minister the sacraments He has given to His Church; and to call people to a love which He has first made possible.

Hence the surrender to God's call can be made with utmost confidence and without reservation. Our surrender to God's will must be total—the "yes" given once for all which has as its pattern the "yes" spoken by Jesus Himself. As St. Paul tells us, "As God keeps his word, I declare that my word to you is not 'yes' one minute and 'no' the next. Jesus Christ...was not alternately 'yes' and 'no'; he was never anything but 'yes' " (1 Cor. 1:18-19).

GOD'S GIFT FOR THE CHURCH

This call of God is grace: it is a gift, a treasure "possessed in earthen vessels to make it clear that its surpassing power comes from God and not from us" (2 Cor. 4:7). But this gift is not primarily for the priest himself; it is rather a gift of God for the whole Church and for her mission to the world. Priesthood is an abiding sacramental sign which shows that the love of the Good Shepherd for His flock will never be absent. In my letter to you priests last Holy Thursday, I developed this aspect of the priesthood as God's gift: our priesthood, I said, "constitutes a special *ministerium*, that is to say, 'service,' in relation to the community of believers. It does not, however, take its origin from that community, as though it were the community that 'called' or 'delegated.' The sacramental priesthood is truly a gift for this community and comes from Christ Himself, from the fullness of His priesthood" (Letter, 5). In this gift-giving to His people, it is the divine Giver who takes the initiative; it is He who calls the ones "he himself had decided on."

WHY ONLY MALE PRIESTS

Hence when we reflect on the intimacy between the Lord and His prophet, His priest—an intimacy arising as a result of the call which He has initiated— we can better understand certain characteristics of the priesthood and realize their appropriateness for the Church's mission today as well as in times past:

a) Priesthood is forever—*Tu es sacerdos in aeternum*—we do not return the gift once given. It cannot be that God who gave the impulse to say "yes" now wishes to hear "no."

b) Nor should it surprise the world that the call of God through the Church continues to offer us a celibate ministry of love and service after the example of our Lord Jesus Christ. God's call has indeed stirred us to the depths of our being. And after centuries of experience, the Church knows how deeply fitting it is that priests should give this concrete response in their lives to express the totality of the "yes" they have spoken to the Lord who calls them by name to His service.

c) The fact that there is a personal individual call to the priesthood given by the Lord to "the men he himself had decided on" is in accord with the prophetic tradition. It should help us, too, to understand that the Church's traditional decision to call men to the priesthood, and not to call women, is not a statement about human rights, nor an exclusion of women from holiness and mission in the Church. Rather this decision expresses the conviction of the Church about this particular dimension of the gift of priesthood by which God has chosen to shepherd His flock.

MISSION AND SERVICE

3. Dear brothers: "God's flock is in your midst; give it a shepherd's care." How close to the essence of our understanding of priesthood is the role of shepherd; throughout the history of salvation it is a recurring image of God's care for His people. And only in the role of Jesus, the Good Shepherd, can our pastoral ministry as priests be understood. Recall how, in the call of the Twelve, Jesus summoned them to be His companions precisely in order to "send them out to preach the good news." Priesthood is mission and service; it is being "sent out" from Jesus to "give His flock a shepherd's care." This characteristic of the priest—to apply an excellent phrase about Jesus as the "man-for-others"—shows us the true sense of what it means to "give a shepherd's care." It means pointing

the awareness of humanity to the mystery of God, to the profundity of redemption taking place in Christ Jesus. Priestly ministry is missionary in its very core: it means being sent out for others, like Christ sent from His Father, for the sake of the Gospel, sent to evangelize. In the words of Paul VI, "Evangelizing means bringing the Good News into all the strata of humanity...and making it new" (*Evangelii nuntiandi,* 18). At the foundation and center of its dynamism, evangelization contains a clear proclamation that salvation is in Jesus Christ, the Son of God. It is His name, His teaching, His life, His promises, His kingdom and His mystery that we proclaim to the world. And the effectiveness of our proclamation, and hence the very success of our priesthood, depends on our fidelity to the magisterium, through which the Church guards "the rich deposit of faith with the help of the Holy Spirit who dwells within us" (2 Tm. 1:14).

A MAN FOR OTHERS

As a pattern for every ministry and apostolate in the Church, priestly ministry is never to be conceived in terms of an acquisition; insofar as it is a gift, it is a gift to be proclaimed and shared with others. Do we not see this clearly in Jesus' teaching when the mother of James and John asked that her sons sit on His right hand and His left in His kingdom? "You know how those who exercise authority among the Gentiles lord it over them; their great ones make their importance felt. It cannot be like that with you. Anyone who aspires to greatness must serve the rest, and whoever wants to rank first among you must serve the needs of all. Such is the case with the Son of

Man who has come, not to be served by others, but to serve, to give his own life as a ransom for the many" (Mt. 20:25-28).

Just as Jesus was most perfectly a "man-for-others" in giving Himself up totally on the cross, so the priest is most of all servant and "man-for-others" when he acts *in persona Christi* in the Eucharist, leading the Church in that celebration in which this sacrifice of the cross is renewed. For in the Church's daily Eucharistic worship, the "Good News" that the apostles were sent out to proclaim is preached in its fullness; the work of our redemption is re-enacted.

How perfectly the Fathers of the Second Vatican Council captured this fundamental truth in their *Decree on Priestly Life and Ministry:* "The other sacraments, as every ministry of the Church and every work of the apostolate, are linked with the Holy Eucharist and are directed towards it.... Hence the Eucharist shows itself to be the source and the summit of all evangelization" (*Presbyterorum ordinis,* 5). In the celebration of the Eucharist, we priests are at the very heart of our ministry of service, of "giving God's flock a shepherd's care." All our pastoral endeavors are incomplete until our people are led to the full and active participation in the Eucharistic sacrifice.

UNITY FOR THE SAKE OF THE GOSPEL

4. Let us recall how Jesus named twelve as His companions. The call to priestly service includes an invitation to special intimacy with Christ. The lived experience of priests in every generation has led them to discover in their own lives and ministry the absolute centrality of their personal union with Jesus, of being His companions. No one can effectively bring the Good News of Jesus to others unless he himself has first been His constant companion through personal prayer, unless he has learned from Jesus the mystery to be proclaimed.

This union with Jesus, modeled on His oneness with His Father, has a further intrinsic dimension, as His own prayer at the Last Supper reveals: "That they may be one, Father, even as we are one" (Jn. 17:11). His priesthood is one, and this unity must be actual and effective among His chosen companions. Hence unity among priests, lived out in fraternity and friendship, becomes a demand and an integral part of the life of a priest.

Unity among priests is not a unity or fraternity that is directed towards itself. It is for the sake of the Gospel, to symbolize, in the living out of the priesthood, the essential direction to which the Gospel calls all people: to the union of love with Him and one another. And this union alone can guarantee peace and justice and dignity to every human being. Surely this is the underlying sense of the prayer of Jesus when He continues: "I pray also for those who believe in me through their word, that all may be one as you, Father, are in me, and I in you" (Jn. 17:20-21). Indeed, how will the world come to believe that the Father has sent Jesus unless people can see in visible ways that those who believe in Jesus have heard His commandment to "love one another"? And how will believers receive a witness that such love is a concrete possibility unless they find it in the example of the unity of their priestly ministers, of those whom Jesus Himself forms into one priesthood as His own companions?

TO GIVE WITNESS

My brother priests: Have we not here touched upon the heart of the matter—our zeal for the priesthood itself? It is inseparable from our zeal for the service of the people. This concelebrated Mass, which so beautifully symbolizes the unity of our priesthood, gives to the whole world the witness of the unity for which Jesus prayed to His Father on our behalf. But it must not become a merely transient manifestation, which would render fruitless the prayer of Jesus.

Every Eucharist renews this prayer for our unity: "Lord, remember your Church throughout the world; make us grow in love, together with John Paul, our Pope,...our Bishop, and all the clergy."

Your priests' senates, as new structures in the Church, provide a wonderful opportunity to give visible witness to the one priesthood you share with your Bishops and with one another, and to demonstrate what must be at the heart of the renewal of every structure in the Church: the unity for which Jesus Himself prayed.

TOTAL SELF-GIVING

5. At the beginning of this homily, I charged you with the task of taking responsibility for your priesthood, a task for each one of you personally, a charge to be shared with all the priests, and especially to be a concern for your priests' councils. The faith of the whole Church needs to have clearly in focus the proper understanding of the priesthood and of its place in the mission of the Church. So the Church depends on you to deepen ever more this understanding, and to put it into practice in your lives and ministry: in other words, to share the gift of your priesthood with the Church by renewing the response you have already made to Christ's invitation—"Come, follow me"—by giving yourselves as totally as He did.

At times we hear the words, "pray for priests." And today I address these words as an appeal, as a plea, to all the faithful of the Church in the United States. Pray for priests, so that each and every one of them will repeatedly say *yes* to the call he has received, remain constant in preaching the Gospel message, and be faithful forever as the companion of our Lord Jesus Christ.

Dear brother priests: As we renew the Paschal Mystery and stand as disciples at the foot of the cross with Mary, the Mother of Jesus, let us entrust ourselves to her. In her love we shall find strength for our weakness and joy for our hearts.

CLOSE TO
GOD'S NATURE

On October 4, from Philadelphia the Pope traveled by air to Des Moines, Iowa, an important agricultural center of the Midwest. The Holy Father's brief stop in this city indicated the Church's solicitude for the farming communities and to call attention to the grave food problems throughout the world. After a welcome in Des Moines by the civic and religious leaders of the state and city, the Pope left at once for the small parish of St. Patrick where, to the parishioners gathered in the church, he spoke as follows:

Dear brothers and sisters,

It gives me great pleasure to be here today with you, in the heartland of America, in this lovely St. Patrick's Church at the Irish Settlement. My pastoral journey through the United States would have seemed incomplete without a visit, although short, to a rural community like this. Let me share with you some thoughts that this particular setting brings to mind, and that are prompted by my meeting with the families who make up this rural parish.

To proclaim Jesus Christ and His Gospel is the fundamental task which the Church has received from her Founder, and which she has taken up ever since the dawn of the first Pentecost. The early Christians were faithful to this mission which the Lord Jesus gave them through His apostles: "They devoted themselves to the apostles' teaching and fellowship, to the breaking of the bread and the prayers" (Acts 2:42). This is what every community of believers

must do: proclaim Christ and His Gospel in fellow-ship and apostolic faith, in prayer and in the celebration of the Eucharist.

How many Catholic parishes have been started like yours in the early beginnings of the settlement of this region: a small, unpretentious church at the center of a group of family farms, a place and a symbol of prayer and fellowship, the heart of a real Christian community where people know each other personally, share each other's problems, and give witness together to the love of Jesus Christ.

On your farms you are close to God's nature; in your work on the land you follow the rhythm of the seasons; and in your hearts you feel close to each other as children of a common Father and as brothers and sisters in Christ. How privileged you are, that in such a setting can worship God together, celebrate your spiritual unity and help to carry each other's burdens. The 1974 Synod of Bishops in Rome and Paul VI in his apostolic exhortation *Evangelii nuntiandi* have devoted considerable attention to the small communities where a more human dimension is achieved than is possible in a big city or in a sprawling metropolis. Let your small community be a true place of Christian living and of evangelization, not isolating yourselves from the diocese or from the universal Church, knowing that a community with a human face must also reflect the face of Christ.

Feel grateful to God for the blessings He gives you, not least for the blessing of belonging to this rural parish community. May our heavenly Father bless you, each and every one of you. May the simplicity of your life-style and the closeness of your community be the fertile ground for a growing commitment to Jesus Christ, Son of God and Savior of the world.

I for my part thank the Lord for the opportunity He gave me to come and visit you, and as Vicar of Christ to represent Him in your midst. Thank you also for your warm welcome and for offering me your hospitality as I prepare for my encounter with the larger group of people at the Living Farms.

My gratitude goes in a special way to the Bishop of Des Moines for his most cordial invitation. He pointed out many reasons why a visit to Des Moines would be so meaningful: a city that is one of the major agricultural centers of this country; the headquarters also of the dynamic and deserving Catholic Rural Life Conference, whose history is so closely linked to the name of a pastor and a friend of the rural people, Msgr. Luigi Ligutti; a region distinguished by community involvement and family-centered activity; a diocese that is involved, together with all the Catholic Bishops of the heartland, in a major effort to build community.

My greetings and best wishes go also to the whole state of Iowa, to the civil authorities and to all the people, who have so generously extended to me a hospitality marked by kindness.

May God bless you through the intercession of Mary, the Mother of Jesus and the Mother of His Church.

LAND IS GOD'S GIFT ENTRUSTED TO MAN FROM THE VERY BEGINNING

The Holy Father's one-day visit to Des Moines, Iowa, culminated in a Mass in the open at Living History Farms, where about 350,000 persons—the largest crowd in the region's history—cheered, prayed, and listened to the Pope's special message to rural America.

To the large gathering of people, who had begun lining up to get into the farms 12 hours before the opening, the Holy Father delivered the following homily.

Dear brothers and sisters in Christ,

Here in the heartland of America, in the middle of the bountiful fields at harvest time, I come to celebrate the Eucharist. As I stand in your presence in this period of autumn harvest, those words which are repeated whenever people gather for the Eucharist seem to be so appropriate: "Blessed are you, Lord God of all creation, through your goodness we have this bread to offer which earth has given and human hands have made."

As one who has always been close to nature, let me speak to you today about the land, the earth, and that "which earth has given and human hands have made."

GIFT OF GOD

1. The land is God's gift entrusted to people from the very beginning. It is God's gift, given by a loving Creator as a means of sustaining the life which He had created. But the land is not only God's gift; it is also man's responsibility. Man, himself created from the dust of the earth (cf. Gn. 3:7), was made its master (cf. Gn. 1:26). In order to bring forth fruit, the land would depend upon the genius and skillfulness, the sweat and the toil of the people to whom God would entrust it. Thus the food which would sustain life on earth is willed by God to be both that "which earth has given and human hands have made."

To all of you who are farmers and all who are associated with agricultural production I want to say this: the Church highly esteems your work. Christ Himself showed His esteem for agricultural life when He described God His Father as "the vinedresser" (Jn. 15:1). You cooperate with the Creator, the "vinedresser," in sustaining and nurturing life. You fulfill the command of God given at the very beginning: "Fill the earth and subdue it" (Gn. 1:28). Here in the heartland of America, the valleys and hills have been blanketed with grain, the herds and the flocks have multiplied many times over. By hard work you have become masters of the earth and you have subdued it. By reason of the abundant fruitfulness which modern agricultural advances have made possible, you support the lives of millions who themselves do not work on the land, but who live because of what you produce. Mindful of this, I make my own the words of my beloved predecessor, Paul VI: "It is the dignity of those who work on the land and of all those engaged in different levels of research and action in the field of agricultural development which must be unceasingly proclaimed and promoted'' (address to the World Food Conference, Nov. 9, 1974, no. 4).

BLESSING OF CLOSE-KNIT FAMILY

What then are the attitudes that should pervade man's relationship to the land? As always we must look for the answer beginning with Jesus, for, as St. Paul says: "In your minds you must be the same as Christ Jesus" (Phil. 2:5). In the life of Jesus, we see a real closeness to the land. In His teaching, He referred to the "birds of the air" (Mt. 6:26), the "lilies of the field" (Mt. 7:17). He talked about the farmer who went out to sow the seed (Mt. 13:4ff.); and He referred to His heavenly Father as the "vinedresser" (Jn. 15:1), and to Himself as the "good shepherd" (Jn. 10:14). This closeness to nature, this spontaneous awareness of creation as a gift from God, as well as the blessing of a close-knit family—characteristics of farm life in every age including our own—these were part of the life of Jesus. Therefore I invite you to let your attitudes always be the same as those of Christ Jesus.

2. Three attitudes in particular are appropriate for rural life. In the first place: gratitude. Recall the first words of Jesus in the Gospel we have just heard, words of gratitude to His heavenly Father: "Father, Lord of heaven and earth, to you I offer praise." Let this be your attitude as well. Every day the farmer is reminded of how much he depends upon God. From the heavens come the rain, the wind and the sun-

shine. They occur without the farmer's command or control. The farmer prepares the soil, plants the seed, and cultivates the crop. But God makes it grow; He alone is the source of life. Even the natural disasters, such as hailstorms and drought, tornadoes or floods, remind the farmer of his dependence upon God. Surely it was this awareness that prompted the early pilgrims to America to establish the feast which you call "Thanksgiving." After every harvest, whatever it may have been that year, with humility and thankfulness the farmer makes his own the prayer of Jesus: "Father, Lord of heaven and earth, to you I offer praise."

Secondly, the land must be conserved with care since it is intended to be fruitful for generation upon generation. You who live in the heartland of America have been entrusted with some of the earth's best land: the soil so rich in minerals, the climate so favorable for producing bountiful crops, with fresh water and unpolluted air available all around you. You are stewards of some of the most important resources God has given to the world. Therefore conserve the land well, so that your children's children and generations after them will inherit an even richer land than was entrusted to you. But also remember what the heart of your vocation is. While it is true here that farming today provides an economic livelihood for the farmer, still it will always be more than an enterprise of profitmaking. In farming, you cooperate with the Creator in the very sustenance of life on earth.

TO FEED THE HUNGRY OF THE WORLD

In the third place, I want to speak about generosity, a generosity which arises from the fact that "God destined the earth and all it contains for all men and all peoples so that all created things would be shared fairly by all mankind under the guidance of justice tempered by charity" (*Gaudium et spes,* 69). You who are farmers today are stewards of a gift from God which was intended for the good of all humanity. You have the potential to provide food for the millions who have nothing to eat and thus help to rid the world of famine. To you I direct the same question asked by Paul VI five years ago: "...if the potential of nature is immense, if that of the mastery of the human genius over the universe seems almost unlimited, what is it that is too often missing...except that generosity, that anxiety which is stimulated by the sight of the sufferings and the miseries of the poor, that deep conviction that the whole family suffers when one of its members is in distress?'' (Address to the World Food Conference, November 9, 1974, no. 9)

Recall the time when Jesus saw the hungry crowd gathered on the hillside. What was His response? He did not content Himself with expressing His compassion. He gave His disciples the command: "Give them something to eat yourselves" (Mt. 14:16). Did He not intend those same words for us today, for us who live at the closing of the twentieth century, for us who have the means available to feed the hungry of the world? Let us respond generously to His command by sharing the fruit of our labor, by contributing to others the knowledge we have gained, by being the promoters of rural development everywhere and by defending the right to work of the rural population, since every person has a right to useful employment.

CHRIST, THE BREAD THAT SATISFIES

3. Farmers everywhere provide bread for all humanity, but it is Christ alone who is the bread of life. He alone satisfies the deepest hunger of humanity. As St. Augustine said: "Our hearts are restless until they rest in You" (*Confessions* I, 1). While we are mindful of the physical hunger of millions of our brothers and sisters on all continents, at this Eucharist we are reminded that the deepest hunger lies in the human soul. To all who acknowledge this hunger within them Jesus says: "Come to me, all you who are weary and find life burdensome, and I will refresh you." My brothers and sisters in Christ: Let us listen to these words with all our heart. They are directed to

every one of us. To all who till the soil, to all who benefit from the fruit of their labors, to every man and woman on earth, Jesus says: "Come to me...and I will refresh you." Even if all the physical hunger of the world were satisfied, even if everyone who is hungry were fed by his or her own labor or by the generosity of others, the deepest hunger of man would still exist.

We are reminded in the letter of St. Paul to the Galatians: "All that matters is that one is created anew." Only Christ can create one anew; and this new creation finds its beginning only in His cross and resurrection. In Christ alone all creation is restored to its proper order. Therefore, I say: Come, all of you, to Christ. He is the bread of life. Come to Christ and you will never be hungry again.

Bring with you to Christ the products of your hands, the fruit of the land, that "which earth has given and human hands have made." At this altar these gifts will be transformed into the Eucharist of the Lord.

Bring with you your efforts to make fruitful the land, your labor and your weariness. At this altar, because of the life, death and resurrection of Christ, all human activity is sanctified, lifted up and fulfilled.

Bring with you the poor, the sick, the exiled and the hungry; bring all who are weary and find life burdensome. At this altar they will be refreshed, for His yoke is easy and His burden light.

Above all, bring your families and dedicate them anew to Christ, so that they may continue to be the working, living and loving community where nature is revered, where burdens are shared and where the Lord is praised in gratitude.

IN THE NAME OF JESUS
I HAVE COME

After the celebration of Mass at the Living History Farms of Des Moines, the Holy Father, on October 4, departed by plane to Chicago. After an hour's flight the plane landed at O'Hare Airport where the Archbishop of Chicago, Cardinal John Patrick Cody and other high authorities of the city and State awaited him. The first official meeting of the Pope with the priests and faithful of the Archdiocese took place that evening in Holy Name Cathedral.

After listening to an address of welcome by Cardinal Cody, the Holy Father gave the following discourse.

Dear brothers and sisters in Christ,

From Philadelphia to Des Moines, from Des Moines to Chicago! In one day I have seen a great part of your spacious land, and I have thanked God for the faith and the achievements of its people. This evening brings me to Chicago, to Holy Name Cathedral. I am grateful to the Lord for the joy of this encounter.

My special gratitude goes to you, Cardinal Cody, my brother for many years in the College of Bishops, the pastor of this great See of Chicago. I thank you for your kind invitation and for all you have done to prepare for my coming. A greeting of esteem and love goes also to all the priests, both diocesan and religious, who share so particularly and intimately in the responsibility of bringing the message of salvation to all the people. I am likewise looking forward to meet-

ing people from all categories in the Church: deacons and seminarians, religious brothers and women religious, husbands and wives, mothers and fathers, the single, the widowed, the young and the children: so that we can celebrate together our ecclesial unity in Christ.

It is with a special joy that I greet all of you who are present here in Holy Name Cathedral, to which, by God's grace, I return once more. Here there is symbolized and actuated the unity of this archdiocese, this local church—rich in history and in fidelity, rich in generosity to the Gospel, rich in the faith of millions of men, women and children who over the decades have found holiness and justice in our Lord Jesus Christ.

And today I wish to celebrate with you the great mystery expressed in the title of your cathedral: the holy name of Jesus, Son of God and Son of Mary.

I have come to you to speak of salvation in Jesus Christ. I have come to proclaim it anew: to proclaim this message to you and with you and for you—and for all the people. As successor of the apostle Peter speaking in the Holy Spirit, I too proclaim: "There is salvation in no one else, for there is no other name under heaven given by which we must be saved" (Acts 4:12).

It is in the name of Jesus that I come to you. Our service to the needy of the world is exercised in the name of Jesus. Repentance and the forgiveness of sins are preached in His name (cf. Lk. 24:27). And through faith, all of us have "life in his name" (Jn. 20:31).

In this name—in the holy name of Jesus—there is help for the living, consolation for the dying, and joy and hope for the whole world.

With sentiments of admiration and with confidence in your potential for true human greatness, I wish to greet in you the rich variety of your nation, where people of different ethnic origins and creeds can live, work and prosper together in freedom and mutual respect.

Arturo Mari

Above all, a city needs a soul if it is to become a true home for human beings. You, the people, must give it this soul. And how do you do this? By loving each other. Love for each other must be the hallmark of your lives.

Today, by the grace of God, I come here as successor of Peter to bring you a message of love and to strengthen you in your faith. In your kind welcome I feel that you want to honor in me the Christ whom I represent and who lives in all of us.... I feel moreover that I am truly among friends, and I feel very much at home in your midst.

Freedom can therefore never be construed without relation to the truth as revealed by Jesus Christ, and proposed by His Church, nor can it be seen as a pretext for moral anarchy, for every moral order must remain linked to truth.... No freedom can exist when it goes against man in what he is, or against man in his relationship to others and to God.

Curt Clark

One of the things I wanted most to do during my visit to the United States has now arrived. I wanted to visit a seminary and meet the seminarians; and through you I would like to communicate to all seminarians how much you mean to me, and how much you mean for the future of the Church—for the future of the mission given to us by Christ. You hold a special place in my thoughts and prayers.

Myrna Ludwig/Uniphoto/CMS

My brothers and sisters in Christ: this is the lesson we learn from the life of St. John Neumann, and the message which I leave with you today: what really matters in life is that we are loved by Christ, and that we love Him in return. In comparison to the love of Jesus, everything else is secondary. And without the love of Jesus, everything else is useless.

Catholic unity also entails a recognition of the successor of St. Peter and his ministry of strengthening and preserving intact the communion of the universal Church, while safeguarding the existence of legitimate individual traditions within it.

Rev. Michael Gambone

Priesthood is forever—*Tu es sacerdos in aeternum*—we do not return the gift once given. It cannot be that God who gave the impulse to say "yes" now wishes to hear "no."

I for my part thank the Lord for the opportunity He gave me to come and visit you, and as Vicar of Christ to represent Him in your midst. Thank you also for your warm welcome and for offering me your hospitality.

Arturo Mari

How many Catholic parishes have been started like yours in the early beginnings of the settlement of this region: a small, unpretentious church at the center of a group of family farms, a place and a symbol of prayer and fellowship, the heart of a real Christian community where people know each other personally, share each other's problems, and give witness together to the love of Jesus Christ.

Arturo Mari

While we are mindful of the physical hunger of millions of our brothers and sisters on all continents, at this Eucharist we are reminded that the deepest hunger lies in the human soul. To all who acknowledge this hunger within them Jesus says: "Come to me, all you who are weary and find life burdensome, and I will refresh you."

Recall the time when Jesus saw the hungry crowd gathered on the hillside. What was His response? He did not content Himself with expressing His compassion. He gave His disciples the command: "Give them something to eat yourselves" (Mt. 14:16). Did He not intend those same words for us today, for us who live at the closing of the twentieth century, for us who have the means available to feed the hungry of the world?

Michael J. Pettypool/Uniphoto/CMS

The land is God's gift entrusted to people from the very beginning. It is God's gift, given by a loving Creator as a means of sustaining the life which He had created. But the land is not only God's gift; it is also man's responsibility.

Dana Downie/Uniphoto/CMS

Frank E. Smoczynski

   In a while we shall be offering to God bread and wine. I shall accept those gifts from your hands to offer them to the heavenly Father. We do so during every holy Mass. But although we do it each time in the same way, the offering nevertheless each time has another content, it sounds a different voice on our lips and reveals different secrets of our hearts. Today it speaks in a very special way.

His Holiness with Terence Cardinal Cooke of New York (above) and John Cardinal Cody of Chicago (below).

Arturo Mari

His Holiness with Humberto Cardinal Medeiros of Boston (above) and William Cardinal Baum of Washington, D.C. (below).

Arturo M

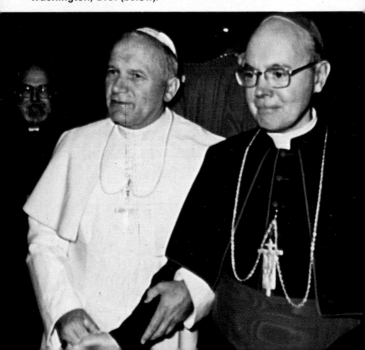

Brothers and sisters in the Church of Chicago: let us do everything "in the name of the Lord Jesus" (Col. 3:12).

May the words which I address to you on my arrival here—coming from him who is called to be the servant of the servants of God—be for all of Chicago, the authorities and the people, an expression of my fraternal solidarity. How greatly I would like to meet each one of you personally, to visit you in your homes, to walk your streets so that I may better understand the richness of your personalities and the depth of your aspirations. May my words to you be an encouragement for all those who strive to bring to your community a sense of brotherhood, dignity, and unity. For in coming here I want to show my respect —beyond the limit of the Catholic Faith, even beyond all religion—for man, for the humanity that is in every human being. The Christ, whom I unworthily represent, taught me to do this. I must obey His command of fraternal love. And I do it with great joy.

May God uplift humanity in this great city of Chicago!

THE HERITAGE OF ST. FRANCIS OF ASSISI

After his meeting with the clergy and faithful of the Archdiocese of Chicago at Holy Name Cathedral, Pope John Paul, on October 4, went to the Church of St. Peter where hundreds of religious had gathered. During the prayer meeting which concluded the Pope's first day in Chicago His Holiness delivered the following address.

Brothers in Christ,

1. "I thank my God whenever I think of you; and every time I pray for you, I pray with joy, remembering how you have helped to spread the good news from the day you first heard it right up to the present" (Phil. 1:3-5). These words of St. Paul express my feelings this evening. It is good to be with you. And I am grateful to God for your presence in the Church and for your collaboration in proclaiming the Good News.

Brothers, Christ is the purpose and the measure of our lives. In the knowledge of Christ, your vocation took its origin; and in His love, your life is sustained. For He has called you to follow Him more closely in a life consecrated through the gift of the evangelical counsels. You follow Him in sacrifice and willing generosity. You follow Him in joy "singing gratefully to God from your hearts in psalms, hymns, and inspired songs" (Col. 3:16). And you follow Him in fidelity, even considering it an honor to suffer humiliation for the sake of His name (cf. Acts 5:42).

Your religious consecration is essentially an act of love. It is an imitation of Christ who gave Himself to

His Father for the salvation of the world. In Christ, the love of His Father and His love for mankind are united. And so it is with you. Your religious consecration has not only deepened your baptismal gift of union with the Trinity, but it has also called you to greater service of the People of God. You are united more closely to the person of Christ, and you share more fully in His mission for the salvation of the world.

It is about your share in the mission of Christ that I wish to speak this evening.

FREE INTERIORLY

2. Let me begin by reminding you of the personal qualities needed to share effectively with Christ in His mission. In the first place, you must be interiorly free, spiritually free. The freedom of which I speak is a paradox to many; it is even misunderstood by some who are members of the Church. Nevertheless it is the fundamental human freedom, and it was won for us by Christ on the cross. As St. Paul said, ''We were still helpless when at his appointed moment Christ died for sinful men'' (Rom. 5:6).

This spiritual freedom which you received in Baptism you have sought to increase and strengthen through your willing acceptance of the call to follow Jesus more closely in poverty, chastity and obedience. No matter what others may contend or the world may believe, your promises to observe the evangelical counsels have not shackled your freedom: you are not less free because you are obedient; and you are not less loving because of your celibacy. On the contrary, the faithful practice of the evangelical counsels accentuates your human dignity, liberates the human heart and causes your spirit to burn with undivided love for Christ and for His brothers and sisters in the world (cf. *Perfectae caritatis*, 1, 12).

But this freedom of an undivided heart (cf. 1 Cor. 7:32-35) must be maintained by continual vigilance and fervent prayer. If you unite yourself continually to Christ in prayer, you shall always be free and ever more eager to share in His mission.

EUCHARIST-CENTERED

3. Secondly, you must center your life around the Eucharist. While you share in many ways in the passion, death and resurrection of Christ, it is especially in the Eucharist where this is celebrated and made effective. At the Eucharist, your spirit is renewed, your mind and heart are refreshed and you will find the strength to live day by day for Him who is the Redeemer of the world.

GOD'S WORD

4. Thirdly, be dedicated to God's Word. Remember the words of Jesus: "My mother and my brothers are those who hear the word of God and put it into practice" (Lk. 8:21). If you sincerely listen to God's Word, and humbly but persistently try to put it into practice, like the seed sown in fertile soil, His Word will bear fruit in your life.

FRATERNAL LIFE

5. The fourth and final element which makes effective your sharing in Christ's mission is fraternal life. Your life lived in religious community is the first

concrete expression of love of neighbor. It is there that the first demands of self-sacrifice and generous service are exercised in order to build up the fraternal community. This love which unites you as brothers in community becomes in turn the force which supports you in your mission for the Church.

SEEK HOLINESS

6. Brothers in Christ, today the universal Church honors St. Francis of Assisi. As I think of this great saint, I am reminded of his delight in God's creation, his childlike simplicity, his poetic marriage to "Lady Poverty," his missionary zeal and his desire to share fully in the cross of Christ. What a splendid heritage he has handed on to those among you who are Franciscans, and to all of us.

Similarly, God has raised up many other men and women outstanding in holiness. These, too, He destined to found religious families which, each in a distinctive way, would play an important role in the mission of the Church. The key to the effectiveness of every one of these religious institutes has been their faithfulness to the original charism God had begun in their founder or foundress for the enrichment of the Church. For this reason, I repeat the words of Paul VI. "Be faithful to the spirit of your founders, to their evangelical intentions and to the example of their holiness.... It is precisely here that the dynamism proper to each religious family finds its origin" (*Evangelica testificatio,* 11-12). And this remains a secure basis for judging what specific ecclesial activities each institute, and every individual member, should undertake in order to fulfill the mission of Christ.

7. Never forget the specific and ultimate aim of all apostolic service: to lead the men and women of our day to communion with the Most Holy Trinity. In the present age, mankind is increasingly tempted to seek security in possessions, knowledge and power. By the witness of your life consecrated to Christ in poverty, chastity and obedience, you challenge this false security. You are a living reminder that Christ alone is "the way, the truth and the life" (Jn. 14:6).

ACTIVE APOSTOLATE

8. Religious brothers today are involved in a wide range of activities: teaching in Catholic schools, spreading God's Word in missionary activity, responding to a variety of human needs by both your witness and your actions, and serving by prayer and sacrifice. As you go forward in your particular service, keep in mind the advice of St. Paul: "Whatever you do, work at it with your whole being. Do it for the Lord rather than for men" (Col. 3:23). For the measure of your effectiveness will be the degree of your love for Jesus Christ.

9. Finally, every form of apostolic service, of either an individual or a community, must be in accord with the Gospel as it is put forward by the magisterium. For all Christian service is aimed at spreading the Gospel; and all Christian service incorporates Gospel values. Therefore be men of God's Word: men whose hearts burn within them when they hear the Word proclaimed (cf. Lk. 24:32); who shape every action according to its demands; and who desire to see the Good News proclaimed to the ends of the earth.

Brothers, your presence in the Church and your collaboration in promoting the Gospel are an encouragement and joy to me in my role as Pastor of the whole Church. May God give each of you long life. May He call many others to follow Christ in the religious life. And may the Virgin Mary, Mother of the Church and model of consecrated life, obtain for you the joy and consolation of Christ, her Son.

CONTINUING THE MISSION OF CHRIST IN ASSISTING THE POOR

On the morning of October 5 the Holy Father met those groups which the Campaign for Human Development had assisted and whose representatives were present at the Church of Divine Providence in Chicago. There were present also many inhabitants of the Pilsen quarter, to whom the Pope spoke as follows:

Dear brothers and sisters, dear friends in Christ,

Thank you for your welcome!

I am happy to greet and bless those groups which the Campaign for Human Development has assisted and whose representatives are here today.

This Campaign has been a witness to the Church's living presence in the world among the most needy, and to her commitment to continuing the mission of Christ, who was sent "to bring glad tidings to the poor, to proclaim liberty to the captives,...and release to the prisoners" (Lk. 4:18-19).

I commend the Bishops of the United States for their wisdom and compassion in establishing the Campaign for Human Development ten years ago; and I thank the whole Catholic community for the generous support given to this initiative during all these years.

Nearly 1,500 groups and organizations, I have been told, have received Campaign funding. The efforts aimed at establishing self-help projects deserve praise and encouragement, for in this way an effective contribution is made to removing the causes and not merely the evil effects of injustice. The projects assisted by the Campaign have helped to create a more human and just social order, and they enable many people to achieve an increased measure of rightful self-reliance. They remain in the life of the Church a witness to the love and concern of our Lord Jesus Christ.

May God give you strength, courage and wisdom to continue this work for justice. God bless you all.

The Pope then spoke to the Spanish-speaking group that was present.

Dear Spanish-speaking brothers and sisters,

I am very happy to be here among you in the course of my journey, a short but full one, through this large and beautiful country.

My visit is primarily a pastoral one. It is intended as an invitation to brotherly coexistence and to the peaceful development of good relations between men and peoples, an invitation to seek in Christ the source and the energy in order that God's call to us as men and as Christians may be realized in our lives.

I greatly trust in your prayers, especially in those of children, of old and sick people, and of all those who, through their physical or moral suffering, are closer to Christ, our Savior and Redeemer.

I greet you all with affection and give you my most cordial blessing.

A SPECIAL PRAYER
FOR AMERICAN POLONIA

In a sportsfield adjacent to the school in the parish of Five Holy Martyrs in Chicago, the Pope celebrated Mass for the Polish community of Chicago and delivered the following homily in Polish.

Dear brothers and sisters,

In a while we shall be offering to God bread and wine. I shall accept those gifts from your hands to offer them to the heavenly Father. We do so during every holy Mass. But although we do it each time in the same way, the offering nevertheless each time has another content, it sounds a different voice on our lips and reveals different secrets of our hearts. Today it speaks in a very special way.

By accepting your offertory gifts and placing them on this altar, I would like to express through them all the contributions that the sons and daughters of our first homeland, Poland, have made to the history and to the life of their second homeland across the ocean: all their toil, efforts, struggles and sufferings; all the fruits of their minds, hearts and hands; all the achievements of the individuals, families and communities. But also all the failures, pains and disappointments; all the nostalgia for their homes, when forced by great poverty they went across the ocean; all the price of love they had to part with in order to look here anew for multiplied family, social and ali human threads.

I wish to include in this Eucharistic Sacrifice all the pastoral care of the Church, all the work done by the clergy and by this seminary which has prepared priests through many years; the work of men and especially women religious, who had followed their fellow-countrymen from Poland. And also the activities of various organizations that proved the strength of spirit, the initiative and abilities, and above all the readiness to serve a good cause—a common one, though divided by the ocean between the new and the old homeland.

I have mentioned already here so many things, and I am aware that I have not yet listed them all. And that is why I ask you all, and each one of you: complete the missing items. I would like to place on this altar an offering of everything that you—the American Polonia—have represented from the very beginning, from the time of Kosciuszko and Pulaski throughout the generations, and of everything you represent today.

I wish to offer to God this Holy Sacrifice as a Bishop of Rome and as a Pope who is as well a son of the same nation that you came from.

In this way I wish to fulfill a special obligation: the obligation of my heart and the obligation of history. May Our Lady of Jasna Gora be with us in her maternal way during this holy Sacrifice, as well as the patron saints of our country, whose devotion you have brought over to this land.

May this extraordinary offering of bread and wine, this unique Eucharistic Sacrifice in the story of the American Polonia reunite you in great love and great work. May it enable Jesus Christ to proceed in building your faith and your hope.

FIDELITY TO
THE TRUTH IN LOVE

On the Pope's last day in Chicago, October 5, he met the Bishops of the Episcopal Conference of the United States at Quigley South Seminary, and delivered the following address.

Dear Brothers in our Lord Jesus Christ,

1. May I tell you very simply how grateful I am to you for your invitation to come to the United States. It is an immense joy for me to make this pastoral visit, and in particular, to be here with you today.

On this occasion I thank you, not only for your invitation, not only for everything you have done to prepare for my visit, but also for your partnership in the Gospel from the time of my election as Pope. I thank you for your service to God's holy people, for your fidelity to Christ our Lord, and for your unity with my predecessors and with me in the Church and in the College of Bishops.

I wish at this time to render public homage to a long tradition of fidelity to the Apostolic See on the part of the American hierarchy. During the course of two centuries, this tradition has edified your people, authenticated your apostolate, and enriched the universal Church.

Moreover, in your presence today, I wish to acknowledge with deep appreciation the fidelity of your faithful and the renowned vitality that they have shown in Christian life. This vitality has been manifested not only in the sacramental practice of communities, but also in abundant fruits of the Holy Spirit. With great zeal your people have endeavored to build up the Kingdom of God by means of the Catholic school and through all catechetical efforts. An evident concern for others has been a real part of American Catholicism, and today I thank the American Catholics for their generosity. Their support has benefited the dioceses of the United States, and a widespread network of charitable works and self-help projects, including those sponsored by Catholic Relief Services and the Campaign for Human Development. Moreover, the help given to the missions by the Church in the United States remains a lasting contribution to the cause of Christ's Gospel. Because your faithful have been very generous to the Apostolic See, my predecessors have been assisted in meeting the burdens of their office; and thus, in the exercise of their worldwide mission of charity, they have been able to extend help to those in need, thereby showing the concern of the universal Church for all humanity. For me then this is an hour of solemn gratitude.

AN HOUR OF ECCLESIAL COMMUNION

2. But even more, this is an hour of ecclesial communion and fraternal love. I come to you as a brother Bishop: one who, like yourselves, has known the hopes and challenges of a local church; one who has worked within the structures of a diocese, who has collaborated within the framework of an episcopal conference; one who has known the exhilarating ex

perience of collegiality in an ecumenical council as exercised by Bishops together with him who both presided over this collegial assembly and was recognized by it as *totius ecclesiae pastor*—invested with "full, supreme and universal power over the Church" (*Lumen gentium, 22*). I come to you as one who has been personally edified and enriched by participation in the Synod of Bishops; one who was supported and assisted by the fraternal interest and self-giving of American Bishops who traveled to Poland in order to express solidarity with the Church in my country. I come as one who found deep spiritual consolation for my pastoral activity in the encouragement of Roman Pontiffs with whom, and under whom, I served God's people, and in particular in the encouragement of Paul VI, whom I looked upon not only as head of the College of Bishops, but also as my own spiritual father. And today, under the sign of collegiality and because of a mysterious design of God's Providence, I, your brother in Jesus, now come to you as Successor of Peter in the See of Rome, and therefore as pastor of the whole Church.

Because of my personal pastoral responsibility, and because of our common pastoral responsibility for the People of God in the United States, I desire to strengthen you in your ministry of faith as local pastors, and to support you in your individual and joint pastoral activities by encouraging you to stand fast in the holiness and truth of our Lord Jesus Christ. And in you I desire to honor Jesus Christ, the Shepherd and Bishop of our souls (cf. 1 Pt. 2:25).

Because we have been called to be shepherds of the flock, we realize that we must present ourselves as humble servants of the Gospel. Our leadership will be effective only to the extent that our own discipleship is genuine—to the extent that the beatitudes have become the inspiration of our lives, to the extent that our people really find in us the kindness, simplicity of life and universal charity that they expect.

We who, by divine mandate, must proclaim the duties of the Christian law, and who must call our people to constant conversion and renewal, know that St. Paul's invitation applies above all to ourselves: "You must put on the new man created in God's image, whose justice and holiness are born of truth" (Eph. 4:24).

PERSONAL CONVERSION

3. The holiness of personal conversion is indeed the condition for our fruitful ministry as Bishops of the Church. It is our union with Jesus Christ that determines the credibility of our witness to the Gospel and the supernatural effectiveness of our activity. We can convincingly proclaim "the unsearchable riches of Christ" (Eph. 3:8) only if we maintain fidelity to the love and friendship of Jesus, only if we continue to live in the faith of the Son of God.

God has given a great gift to the American hierarchy in recent years: the canonization of John Neumann. An American Bishop is officially held up by the Catholic Church to be an exemplary servant of the Gospel and shepherd of God's people, above all because of his great love of Christ. On the occasion of the canonization, Paul VI asked: "What is the meaning of this extraordinary event, the meaning of this canonization?" And he answered, saying: "It is the celebration of holiness." And this holiness of St. John Neumann

was expressed in brotherly love, in pastoral charity, and in zealous service by one who was the Bishop of a diocese and an authentic disciple of Christ.

During the canonization, Paul VI went on to say: "Our ceremony today is indeed the celebration of holiness. At the same time, it is a prophetic anticipation—for the Church, for the United States, for the world—of a renewal of love: love for God, love for neighbor." As Bishops, we are called to exercise in the Church this prophetic role of love and, therefore, of holiness.

Guided by the Holy Spirit, we must all be deeply convinced that holiness is the first priority in our lives and in our ministry. In this context, as Bishops we see the immense value of prayer: the liturgical prayer of the Church, our prayer together, our prayer alone. In recent times many of you have found that the practice of making spiritual retreats together with your brother Bishops is indeed a help to that holiness born of truth. May God sustain you in this initiative so that each of you, and all of you together, may fulfill your role as a sign of holiness offered to God's people on their pilgrimage to the Father. May you yourselves, like St. John Neumann, also be a prophetic anticipation of holiness. The people need to have Bishops whom they can look upon as leaders in the quest for holiness—Bishops who are trying to anticipate prophetically in their own lives the attainment of the goal to which they are leading the faithful.

CONSECRATED IN TRUTH

4. St. Paul points out the relationship of justice and holiness to truth (cf. Eph. 4:24). Jesus Himself, in His priestly prayer, asks His Father to consecrate His

disciples by means of truth; and He adds: "Your word is truth"—*sermo tuus veritas est* (Jn. 17:17). And He goes on to say that He consecrates Himself for the sake of the disciples, so that they themselves may be consecrated in truth. Jesus consecrated Himself so that the disciples might be consecrated, set apart, by the communication of what He was: the truth. Jesus tells His Father: "I gave them your word"—"your word is truth" (Jn. 17:14, 17).

The holy Word of God, which is truth, is communicated by Jesus to His disciples. This Word is entrusted as a sacred deposit to His Church, but only after He had implanted in His Church, through the power of the Holy Spirit, a special charism to guard and transmit intact the Word of God.

With great wisdom, John XXIII convoked the Second Vatican Council. Reading the signs of the times, he knew that what was needed was a council of a pastoral nature, a council that would reflect the great pastoral love and care of Jesus Christ, the Good Shepherd, for His people. But he knew that a pastoral council—to be genuinely effective—would need a strong doctrinal basis. And precisely for this reason, precisely because the Word of God is the only basis for every pastoral initiative, John XXIII on the opening day of the Council—October 11, 1962—made the following statement: "The greatest concern of the ecumenical council is this: that the sacred deposit of Christian doctrine should be more effectively guarded and taught."

This explains Pope John's inspiration; this is what the new Pentecost was to be: this is why the Bishops of the Church—in the greatest manifestation of col-

legiality in the history of the world—were called together: "so that the sacred deposit of Christian doctrine should be more effectively guarded and taught."

In our time, Jesus was consecrating anew His
disciples by truth; and He was doing it by means of an
ecumenical council; He was transmitting by the
power of the Holy Spirit His Father's Word to new
generations. And, what John XXIII considered to be
the aim of the Council, I consider as the aim of this
postconciliar period.

SAFEGUARD DOCTRINE

For this reason, in my first meeting last November with American Bishops on their *ad limina* visit I
stated: "This then is my own deepest hope today for
the pastors of the Church in America, as well as for all
the pastors of the universal Church: that the sacred
deposit of Christian doctrine should be more effectively guarded and taught." In the Word of God is the
salvation of the world. By means of the proclamation
of the Word of God, the Lord continues in His Church
and through His Church to consecrate His disciples,
communicating to them the truth that He Himself is.

For this reason the Vatican Council emphasized
the Bishop's role of announcing the full truth of the
Gospel and proclaiming "the whole mystery of
Christ" (*Christus Dominus*, 12). This teaching was constantly repeated by Paul VI for the edification of the
universal Church. It was explicitly proclaimed by
John Paul I on the very day he died, and I too have frequently reaffirmed it in my own pontificate. And I am
sure that my successors and your successors will hold
this teaching until Christ comes again in glory.

"I AM RESOLVED"

5. Among the papers that were left to me by Pope Paul VI there is a letter written to him by a Bishop, on the occasion of the latter's appointment to the episcopacy. It is a beautiful letter; and in the form of a resolution it includes a clear affirmation of the Bishop's role of guarding and teaching the deposit of Christian doctrine, of proclaiming the whole mystery of Christ. Because of the splendid insights that this letter offers, I would like to share part of it with you.

As he pledged himself to be loyal and obedient to Paul VI and to his successors, the Bishop wrote: "I am resolved:

—"To be faithful and constant in proclaiming the Gospel of Christ.

—"To maintain the content of faith, entire and uncorrupted, as handed down by the apostles and professed by the Church at all times and places."

And then with equal insight, this Bishop went on to tell Paul VI that, with the help of Almighty God, he was determined:

—"To build up the Church as the Body of Christ, and to remain united to it by your link, with the order of Bishops, under the authority of the successor of St. Peter the Apostle.

—"To show kindness and compassion in the name of the Lord to the poor and to strangers and to all who are in need.

—"To seek out the sheep who stray and to gather them into the fold of the Lord.

—"To pray without ceasing for the People of God, to carry out the highest duties of the priesthood in such a way as to afford no grounds for reproof."

This then is the edifying witness of a Bishop, an American Bishop, to the episcopal ministry of holiness and truth. These words are a credit to him and a credit to all of you.

A challenge for our age—and for every age in the Church—is to bring the message of the Gospel to the very core of our people's lives—so that they may live the full truth of their humanity, their redemption and their adoption in Jesus Christ—that they may be enriched with "the justice and holiness of truth."

RELEVANCE OF GOD'S WORD

6. In the exercise of your ministry of truth, as Bishops of the United States, you have, through statements and pastoral letters, collectively offered the Word of God to your people, showing its relevance to daily life, pointing to the power it has to uplift and heal, and at the same time upholding its inherent demands. Three years ago you did this in a very special way through your pastoral letter, so beautifully entitled "To Live in Christ Jesus." This letter, in which you offered your people the service of truth, contains a number of points to which I wish to allude today. With compassion, understanding and love, you transmitted a message that is linked to Revelation and to the mystery of faith. And so with great pastoral charity you spoke of God's love, of humanity and of sin—and of the meaning of redemption and of life in Christ. You spoke of the word of Christ as it affects individuals, the family, the community and nations. You spoke of justice and peace, of charity, of truth and friendship. And you spoke of some special questions affecting the moral life of Christians: the moral life in both its individual and social aspects.

You spoke explicitly of the Church's duty to be faithful to the mission entrusted to her. And precisely for this reason you spoke of certain issues that needed a clear reaffirmation, because Catholic teaching in their regard had been challenged, denied, or in practice violated.

You repeatedly proclaimed human rights and human dignity and the incomparable worth of people of every racial and ethnic origin, declaring that "racial antagonism and discrimination are among the most persistent and destructive evils of our nation." You forcefully rejected the oppression of the weak, the manipulation of the vulnerable, the waste of goods and resources, the ceaseless preparations for war, unjust social structures and policies and all crimes by and against individuals and against creation.

DIVORCE, CONTRACEPTION, HOMOSEXUALITY

With the candor of the Gospels, the compassion of pastors and the charity of Christ, you faced the question of the indissolubility of marriage, rightly stating: "The covenant between a man and a woman joined in Christian marriage is as indissoluble and irrevocable as God's love for His people and Christ's love for His Church."

In exalting the beauty of marriage you rightly spoke against both the ideology of contraception and contraceptive acts, as did the encyclical *Humanae vitae*. And I myself today, with the same conviction of Paul VI, ratify the teaching of this encyclical, which was put forth by my predecessor "by virtue of the mandate entrusted to us by Christ" (*AAS*, 60, 1968, p. 485).

In portraying the sexual union between husband and wife as a special expression of their covenanted love, you rightly stated: "Sexual intercourse is a moral and human good only within marriage, outside marriage it is wrong."

As "men with the message of truth and the power of God" (2 Cor. 6:7), as authentic teachers of God's law and as compassionate pastors you also rightly stated: "Homosexual activity,...as distinguished from homosexual orientation, is morally wrong." In the clarity of this truth, you exemplified the real charity of Christ; you did not betray those people who, because of homosexuality, are confronted with difficult moral problems, as would have happened if, in the name of understanding and compassion, or for any other reason, you had held out false hope to any brother or sister. Rather, by your witness to the truth of humanity in God's plan, you effectively manifested fraternal love, upholding the true dignity, the true human dignity, of those who look to Christ's Church for the guidance which comes from the light of God's word.

RIGHT TO LIFE OF THE UNBORN

You also gave witness to the truth, thereby serving all humanity, when, echoing the teaching of the Council—"From the moment of conception life must be guarded with the greatest care" (*Gaudium et spes*, 51)—you reaffirmed the right to life and the inviolability of every human life, including the life of unborn children. You clearly said: "To destroy these innocent unborn children is an unspeakable crime.... Their right to life must be recognized and fully protected by the law."

And just as you defended the unborn in the truth of their being, so also you clearly spoke up for the aged, asserting, "Euthanasia or mercy killing...is a grave moral evil.... Such killing is incompatible with respect for human dignity and reverence for life."

And in your pastoral interest for your people in all their needs—including housing, education, health care, employment, and the administration of justice —you gave further witness to the fact that all aspects of human life are sacred. You were, in effect, proclaiming that the Church will never abandon man, nor his temporal needs, as she leads humanity to salvation and eternal life. And because the Church's greatest act of fidelity to humanity and her "fundamental function in every age and particularly in ours is to direct man's gaze, to point the awareness and experience of the whole of humanity toward the mystery of God" (*Redemptor hominis*, 10)—because of this you rightly alluded to the dimension of eternal life. It is indeed in this proclamation of eternal life that we hold up a great motive of hope for our people against the onslaughts of materialism, against rampant secularism and against moral permissiveness.

RESPONSIBLE PASTORAL INITIATIVES

7. A sense of pastoral responsibility has also been genuinely expressed by individual Bishops in their ministry as local pastors. To the great credit of their authors I would cite but two recent examples of pastoral letters issued in the United States. Both are examples of responsible pastoral initiatives. One of them deals with the issue of racism and vigorously de-

nounces it. The other refers to homosexuality and deals with the issue, as should be done, with clarity and great pastoral charity, thus rendering a real service to truth and to those who are seeking this liberating truth.

Brothers in Christ: as we proclaim the truth in love, it is not possible for us to avoid all criticism; nor is it possible to please everyone. But it is possible to work for the real benefit of everyone. And so we are humbly convinced that God is with us in our ministry of truth, and that He "did not give us a spirit of timidity but a spirit of power and love and self-control" (2 Tim. 1:7).

One of the greatest rights of the faithful is to receive the Word of God in its purity and integrity as guaranteed by the magisterium of the universal Church: the authentic magisterium of the Bishops of the Catholic Church teaching in union with the Pope. Dear brothers: we can be assured that the Holy Spirit is assisting us in our teaching if we remain absolutely faithful to the universal magisterium.

In this regard I wish to add an extremely important point which I recently emphasized in speaking to a group of Bishops making their *ad limina* visit: "In the community of the faithful—which must always maintain Catholic unity with the Bishops and the Apostolic See—there are great insights of faith. The Holy Spirit is active in enlightening the minds of the faithful with His truth, and in inflaming their hearts with His love. But these insights of faith and this *sensus fidelium* are not independent of the magisterium of the Church, which is an instrument of the same Holy Spirit and is assisted by Him. It is only when the faithful have been nourished by the Word of God, faithfully transmitted in its purity and integrity, that their own charisms are fully operative and fruitful. Once the Word of God is faithfully proclaimed to the community and is accepted, it brings forth fruits of justice and holiness of life in abundance. But the dynamism of the community in understanding and living the Word of God depends on its receiving intact the *depositum fidei;* and for this precise purpose a special apostolic and pastoral charism has been given to the Church It is one and the same Spirit of truth who directs the hearts of the faithful and who guarantees the magisterium of the pastors of the flock.''

CUSTODIANS OF THE CHURCH'S UNITY

8. One of the greatest truths of which we are the humble custodians is the doctrine of the Church's unity—that unity which is tarnished on the human face of the Church by every form of sin, but which subsists indestructibly in the Catholic Church (cf. *Lumen gentium,* 8; *Unitatis redintegratio,* 2, 3). A consciousness of sin calls us incessantly to conversion. The will of Christ impels us to work earnestly and perseveringly for unity with all our Christian brethren, being mindful that the unity we seek is one of perfect faith, a unity in truth and love. We must pray and study together, knowing, however, that intercommunion between divided Christians is not the answer to Christ's appeal for perfect unity. And with God's help we will continue to work humbly and resolutely to remove the real divisions that still exist, and thus to restore that full unity in faith which is the condition for sharing in the Eucharist (cf. Address of

May 4, 1979). The commitment of the ecumenical council belongs to each of us; as does the testament of Paul VI, who writing on ecumenism stated: "Let the work of drawing near to our separated brethren go on, with much understanding, with much patience, with great love; but without deviating from the true Catholic doctrine."

SACRAMENT OF PENANCE AND GENERAL ABSOLUTION

9. As Bishops who are servants of truth, we are also called to be servants of unity, in the communion of the Church.

In the communion of holiness we ourselves are called, as I mentioned above, to conversion, so that we may preach with convincing power the message of Jesus: "Reform your lives and believe in the Gospel." We have a special role to play in safeguarding the sacrament of reconciliation, so that, in fidelity to a divine precept, we and our people may experience in our innermost being that "grace has far surpassed sin" (Rom. 5:20).

I, too, ratify the prophetic call of Paul VI, who urged the Bishops to help their priests to "deeply understand how closely they collaborate through the sacrament of Penance with the Savior in the work of conversion" (Address of April 20, 1978). In this regard I confirm again the norms of *Sacramentum paenitentiae* which so wisely emphasize the ecclesial dimension of the sacrament of Penance and indicate the precise limits of general absolution, just as Paul VI did in his *ad limina* address to the American Bishops.

Conversion by its very nature is the condition for that union with God which reaches its greatest ex-

pression in the Eucharist. Our union with Christ in the Eucharist presupposes, in turn, that our hearts are set on conversion, that they are pure. This is indeed an important part of our preaching to the people. In my encyclical I endeavored to express it in these words: ''The Christ who calls to the Eucharistic banquet is always the same Christ who exhorts us to penance and repeats His 'repent.' Without this constant and ever-renewed endeavor for conversion, partaking of the Eucharist would lack its full redeeming effectiveness...'' (*Redemptor hominis,* 20). In the face of a widespread phenomenon of our time, namely, that many of our people who are among the great numbers who receive Communion make little use of confession, we must emphasize Christ's basic call to conversion. We must also stress that the personal encounter with the forgiving Jesus in the sacrament of Reconciliation is a divine means which keeps alive in our hearts and in our communities, a consciousness of sin in its perennial and tragic reality, and which actually brings forth, by the action of Jesus and the power of His Spirit, fruits of conversion in justice and holiness of life. By this sacrament we are renewed in fervor, strengthened in our resolves and buoyed up by divine encouragement.

CHRIST'S REAL PRESENCE IN THE EUCHARIST

10. As chosen leaders in a community of praise and prayer, it is our special joy to offer the Eucharist and to give our people a sense of their vocation as an Easter people, with the ''Alleluia'' as their song. And let us always recall that the validity of all liturgical de-

velopment and the effectiveness of every liturgical sign presupposes the great principle that the Catholic liturgy is theocentric, and that it is above all "the worship of Divine Majesty" (cf. *Sacrosanctum concilium,* 33), in union with Jesus Christ. Our people have a supernatural sense whereby they look for reverence in all liturgy, especially in what touches the mystery of the Eucharist. With deep faith our people understand that the Eucharist—in the Mass and outside the Mass—is the Body and Blood of Jesus Christ, and therefore deserves the worship that is given to the living God and to Him alone.

As ministers of a community of service, it is our privilege to proclaim the truth of Christ's union with His members in His Body, the Church. Hence we commend all service rendered in His name and to His brethren (cf. Mt. 25:45).

In a community of witness and evangelization may our testimony be clear and without reproach. In this regard the Catholic press and the other means of social communication are called to fulfill a special role of great dignity at the service of truth and charity. The Church's aim in employing and sponsoring these media is linked to her mission of evangelization and of service to humanity; through the media the Church hopes to promote ever more effectively the uplifting message of the Gospel.

11. And each individual church over which you preside and which you serve is a community founded on the Word of God and acting in the truth of this Word. It is in fidelity to the communion of the universal Church that our local unity is authenticated and made stable. In the communion of the universal Church local churches find their own identity and en-

richment ever more clearly. But all of this requires that the individual churches should maintain complete openness toward the universal Church.

And this is the mystery that we celebrate today in proclaiming the holiness and truth and unity of the episcopal ministry.

Brothers: This ministry of ours makes us accountable to Christ and to His Church. Jesus Christ, the Chief Shepherd (1 Pt. 5:4), loves us and sustains us. It is He who transmits His Father's word and consecrates us in truth, so that each of us may say in turn of our people: "For them I consecrate myself for their sake now, that they may be consecrated in truth" (Jn. 17:19).

Let us pray for and devote special energy to promoting and maintaining vocations to the sacred priesthood, so that the pastoral care of the priestly ministry may be ensured for future generations. I ask you to call upon parents and families, upon priests, religious and laity to unite in fulfilling this vital responsibility of the entire community. And to the young people themselves let us hold up the full challenge of following Christ and of embracing His invitation with full generosity.

As we ourselves pursue every day the justice and holiness born of truth, let us look to Mary, Mother of Jesus, Queen of Apostles, and cause of our joy. May St. Frances Xavier Cabrini, St. Elizabeth Ann Seton and St. John Neumann pray for you, and for all the people whom you are called to serve in holiness and truth and in the unity of Christ and His Church.

Dear brothers: "Grace be with all who love our Lord Jesus Christ with unfailing love" (Eph. 5:24).

BE STRONG
IN THE FAITH

Speaking to the students of the Minor Seminary in Chicago, Pope John Paul II delivered a short address to them as follows:

Dear seminarians,

I extend a special greeting to all of you who are present here today. I want you to know that you have a special place in my thoughts and prayers.

Dear sons in Christ: Be strong in your faith—faith in Christ, and in His Church, faith in all that the Father has revealed and accomplished through His Son and in the Holy Spirit.

During your years in the minor seminary, you have the privilege of studying and deepening your understanding of the faith. Since Baptism you have lived the faith, aided by your parents, your brothers and sisters, and the whole Christian community. And yet today I call upon you to live by faith even more profoundly. For it is faith in God which makes the essential difference in your lives and in the life of every priest.

Be faithful to your daily prayers; they will keep your faith alive and vibrant.

Study the faith diligently so that your knowledge and love of Christ will continually increase.

And nourish your faith each day at Mass, for in the Eucharist we have the source and greatest expression of our faith.

God bless you.

YOU ARE IN A SPECIAL WAY MY BROTHERS AND SISTERS

To a group of sick persons of Chicago who were gathered at Quigley South Seminary, the Holy Father spoke words of love and encouragement.

Dear brothers and sisters,

I have desired to address a heartfelt greeting to all the sick, bedridden and handicapped in the name of the Lord Jesus, who was Himself "a man of suffering, accustomed to infirmity" (Is. 53:3).

I would like to greet you, one by one, to bless you all individually, and to speak to you—to each one of you individually—about Jesus Christ, the one who took upon Himself all human suffering so that He could bring salvation to the whole world. God loves you as His privileged children. For two reasons you are in a very special way my brothers and sisters: because of the love of Christ that binds us together, and particularly because you share so profoundly in the mystery of the cross and the Redemption of Jesus.

Thank you for the suffering you bear in your bodies and your hearts. Thank you for your example of acceptance, of patience and of union with the suffering Christ. Thank you for filling up "what is lacking in the suffering of Christ for the sake of his Body, the Church" (Col. 1:24).

May the peace and the joy of the Lord Jesus be always with you.

YOU ARE WITNESSES
OF UNITY
AS MEMBERS OF
GOD'S PEOPLE

The Holy Father's last meeting with the people of the Chicago area took place at Grant Park which borders Lake Michigan. To the immense gathering of over a million people, Pope John Paul delivered the following homily.

My brothers and sisters in Jesus Christ,

The readings of today's celebration place us immediately before the deep mystery of our calling as Christians.

Before Jesus was taken up to heaven, He gathered His disciples around Him, and He explained to them once more the meaning of His mission of salvation: "Thus it is written"—He said—"that the Messiah must suffer and rise from the dead on the third day. In his name, penance for the remission of sins is to be preached to all nations" (Lk. 24:46-47). At the moment that He took leave of His apostles He commanded them, and through them the whole Church, each one of us: to go out and bring the message of redemption to all nations. St. Paul expresses this forcefully in his second letter to the Corinthians: "He has entrusted the message of reconciliation to us. This makes us ambassadors of Christ. God as it were appealing through us" (2 Cor. 5:19-20).

Once again, the Lord places us fully in the mystery of humanity, a humanity that is in need of salvation. And God has willed that the salvation of humanity should take place through the humanity of Christ, who for our sake died and was raised up (cf. 2 Cor. 5:15), and who also entrusted His redeeming mission to us. Yes, we are truly "ambassadors for Christ," and workers for evangelization.

In the Apostolic Exhortation *Evangelii nuntiandi,* which he wrote at the request of the Third General Assembly of the Synod of Bishops, my predecessor in the See of St. Peter, Paul VI, invited the whole People of God to meditate on their basic duty of evangelization. He invited each one of us to examine in what way we might be true witnesses to the message of redemption, in what way we might communicate to others the Good News that we have received from Jesus through His Church.

There are certain conditions that are necessary if we are to share in the evangelizing mission of the Church. This afternoon, I wish to stress one of these conditions in particular. I am speaking about the unity of the Church, our unity in Jesus Christ. Let me repeat what Paul VI said about this unity: "The Lord's spiritual testament tells us that unity among His followers is not only the proof that we are His, but also the proof that He is sent by the Father. It is the test of credibility of Christians and of Christ Himself.... Yes, the destiny of evangelization is certainly bound up with the witness of unity given by the Church" (*Evangelii nuntiandi,* 77).

I am prompted to choose this particular aspect of evangelization by looking at the thousands of people whom I see gathered around me today. When I lift up

my eyes, I see in you the People of God, united to sing the praises of the Lord and to celebrate His Eucharist. I see also the whole people of America, one nation formed of many people: *E pluribus unum*.

In the first two centuries of your history as a nation, you have travelled a long road, always in search of a better future, in search of stable employment, in search of a homestead. You have travelled "From sea to shining sea" to find your identity, to discover each other along the way, and to find your own place in this immense country.

Your ancestors came from many different countries across the oceans to meet here with the people of different communities that were already established here. In every generation, the process has been repeated: new groups arrive, each one with a different history, to settle here and become part of something new. The same process still goes on when families move from the south to the north, from the east to the west. Each time they come with their own past to a new town or a new city, to become part of a new community. The pattern repeats itself over and over: *E pluribus unum*—the many form a new unity.

Yes, something new was created every time. You brought with you a different culture and you contributed your own distinctive richness to the whole; you had different skills and you put them to work, complementing each other, to create industry, agriculture and business; each group carried with it different human values and shared them with the others for the enrichment of your nation. *E pluribus unum:* you became a new entity, a new people, the true nature of which cannot be adequately explained as a mere putting together of various communities.

And so, looking at you, I see people who have thrown their destinies together and now write a common history. Different as you are, you have come to accept each other, at times imperfectly and even to the point of subjecting each other to various forms of discrimination; at times only after a long period of misunderstanding and rejection; even now still growing in understanding and appreciation of each other's differences. In expressing gratitude for the many blessings you have received, you also become aware of the duty you have towards the less favored in your own midst and in the rest of the world—a duty of sharing, of loving, of serving. As a people, you recognize God as the source of your many blessings, and you are open to His love and His law.

This is America in her ideal and her resolution: "one nation, under God, indivisible, with liberty and justice for all." This is the way America was conceived: this is what she was called to be. And for all this, we offer thanks to the Lord.

But there is another reality that I see when I look at you. It is even deeper, and more demanding than the common history and union which you built from the richness of your different cultural and ethnic heritages—those heritages that you now rightly want to know and to preserve. History does not exhaust itself in material progress, in technological conquest, or in cultural achievement only. Coming together around the altar of sacrifice to break the Bread of the Holy Eucharist with the Successor of Peter, you testify to this even deeper reality: to your unity as members of the People of God.

"We, though many, are one body in Christ" (Rom. 12:5). The Church too is composed of many members and enriched by the diversity of those who make up the one community of faith and Baptism, the one Body of Christ. What brings us together and makes us one is our faith—the one apostolic faith. We are all one, because we have accepted Jesus Christ as the Son of God, the Redeemer of the human race, the sole Mediator between God and man. By the sacrament of Baptism we have been truly incorporated into the crucified and glorified Christ, and through the action of the Holy Spirit we have become living members of His one body. Christ gave us the wonderful sacrament of the Eucharist, by which the unity of the Church is both expressed and continually brought about and perfected.

"One Lord, one faith, one baptism" (Eph. 4:5), thus we are all bound together, as the People of God, the Body of Christ, in a unity that transcends the diversity of our origin, culture, education and personality—in a unity that does not exclude a rich diversity in ministries and services. With St. Paul we proclaim: "Just as each of us has one body with many members, and not all the members have the same function, so too we, though many, are one body in Christ, and individually members one of another" (Rom. 12:4-5).

If then the Church, the one Body of Christ, is to be a forcefully discernible sign of the Gospel message, all her members must show forth, in the words of Paul VI, that "harmony and consistency of doctrine, life and worship which marked the first day of her existence" (*Apostolic Exhortation on Reconciliation within the Church,* 2), when Christians "devoted themselves to the apostles' teaching and fellowship, to the breaking of bread and the prayers" (Acts 2:42).

Our unity in faith must be complete, lest we fail to give witness to the Gospel, lest we cease to be evangelizing. No local ecclesial community therefore can cut itself off from the treasure of the faith as proclaimed by the Church's teaching office, for it is to this teaching office of the Church, to this Magisterium that the deposit of faith has been especially entrusted by Christ. With Paul VI I attest to the great truth: "While being translated into all expressions, the content of the faith must be neither impaired nor mutilated. While being clothed with the outward forms proper to each people...it must remain the content of the Catholic faith just exactly as the ecclesial Magisterium has received it and transmits it" (*Evangelii nuntiandi*, 65).

Finally, and above all, the mission of evangelization that is mine and yours, must be carried out through a constant unselfish witnessing to the unity of love. Love is the force that opens hearts to the word of Jesus and to His redemption: love is the only basis of human relationships that respect in one another the dignity of the children of God created in His image and saved by the death and resurrection of Jesus; love is the only driving force that impels us to share with our brothers and sisters all that we are and have.

Love is the power that gives rise to dialogue, in which we listen to each other and learn from each other. Love gives rise, above all, to the dialogue of prayer in which we listen to God's word, which is alive in the Holy Bible and alive in the life of the Church. Let love then build the bridges across our differences and at times our contrasting positions. Let love for each other and love for truth be the answer to polarization, when factions are formed because of differing views in matters that relate to faith or to the priorities for action. No one in the ecclesial community should ever feel alienated or unloved, even when tensions arise in the course of the common efforts to bring the fruits of the Gospel to society around us. Our unity as Christians, as Catholics, must always be a unity of love in Jesus Christ our Lord.

In a few moments, we shall celebrate our unity by renewing the sacrifice of Christ. Each one will bring a different gift to be presented in union with the offering of Jesus: dedication to the betterment of society; efforts to console those who suffer; the desire to give witness for justice; the resolve to work for peace and brotherhood; the joy of a united family; or suffering in body or mind. Different gifts, yes, but all united in the one great gift of Christ's love for His Father and for us—everything united in the unity of Christ and His sacrifice.

And in the strength and power, in the joy and peace of this sacred unity, we pledge ourselves anew—as one people—to fulfill the command of our Lord Jesus Christ: Go and teach all people my Gospel. By word and example give witness to my name. And, behold, I am with you always, until the end of the world.

POPE'S GREETING
TO ALL ARTISTS
OF THE LAND

Chicago's Symphony Orchestra offered a final tribute and farewell to His Holiness, John Paul II, with a concert in his honor on the evening of October 5, in the Church of the Holy Name. The orchestra offered a superb presentation of the Fifth Symphony by the Austrian composer Anton Bruckner, at the close of which the Holy Father gave the following address.

I am indeed honored by the splendid performance of the Chicago Symphony Orchestra.

I thank you for the opportunity to express my profound admiration for the artistic beauty which you have shared with me tonight. Please accept my deep gratitude.

And I am honored to be able, on this occasion, to join my voice to that of my predecessor Paul VI, who through the eloquent testimony of a long pontificate, showed himself to be the friend of artists. With all the intensity of his noble soul, he convincingly attested to the Church's esteem for the role of art. With consummate skill himself, he led the Catholic Church to a new level of dialogue with the artists of the world. It was his fond hope that all art and beauty would lift the gaze of man toward God, pointing the way to uncreated beauty.

For the honor of the memory of Paul VI, in my own name, and on behalf of the Church, I reiterate my respect and admiration for your uplifting contribution to humanity, for your artistic creation that exalts what is human and reaches what is religious and divine.

In the cultural and spiritual encounter of this evening, I extend my respectful greetings to all the artists of this land, extolling the role they are called to play, with prodigious capacity, for the advancement of true culture in the United States and in the whole world.

MY CORDIAL GREETING TO THE AMERICAN PEOPLE

The Holy Father arrived at Andrews Military Air Base on Saturday morning, October 6, and was received by the Archbishop of Washington, Cardinal Baum; Mr. Walter Mondale, Vice-President of the United States; Mr. Cyrus Vance, Secretary of State; Mr. Brzezinsky, Presidential adviser on security; and the governor of Maryland, Mr. Hughes. To the assembled group the Holy Father spoke as follows.

Mr. Vice-President, dear friends, dear brothers and sisters in Christ,

I wish to express my sincere thanks for the gracious words of welcome that have been extended to me on my arrival at the nation's Capital, the last stage of my first apostolic journey to the United States. I wish to say once more how grateful I am for the invitation of the Episcopal Conference and of President Carter to come and visit the United States.

I extend a cordial greeting to all those who have come to welcome me here: to you, Mr. Vice-President, and to the other civil authorities, in whom I greet the whole American people and in a particular way all the citizens of the Federal District of Columbia. A fraternal greeting to you, Cardinal Baum, pastor of the Archdiocese of Washington, and through you to all the clergy, religious and laity of the Catholic community. I am most happy to greet at the same time the president, officers and staff of the National Conference of Catholic Bishops that has its headquarters in this city, as well as all those who in the United States Catholic Conference provide all the indispensable services to the whole Catholic community of this country. To all my brother Bishops, a greeting and a blessing from the Bishop of Rome in the See of St. Peter, for you and your dioceses.

I am looking forward to meeting the leaders of this young and flourishing country—in the first place, the President of the United States. I shall also be honored to visit the headquarters of the Organization of American States to bring to this deserving body a message of peace for all the peoples who are represented here.

It will give me a special pleasure, during these last days of my visit and pilgrimage, to come into contact with the Catholic community of this area, and to learn about their pastoral efforts, programs and activities.

May the blessings of aimighty God descend in abundance on all the people of this nation's Capital.

MARY IS THE MODEL OF THE CHURCH

After a brief rest at the Reflecting Pool during which the Holy Father received the official welcome of the Mayor of Washington, Marion Barry, he went to St. Matthew's Cathedral where some 1,400 priests, deacons and lay members of the archdiocesan council awaited him. During the Eucharistic celebration the Pope delivered the following homily.

Mary says to us today: "I am the servant of the Lord. Let it be done to me as you say" (Lk. 1:38).

And with those words, she expresses what was the fundamental attitude of her life: her faith! Mary believed! She trusted in God's promises and was faithful to His will. When the angel Gabriel announced that she was chosen to be the Mother of the Most High, she gave her "Fiat" humbly and with full freedom: "Let it be done to me as you say."

Perhaps the best description of Mary and, at the same time the greatest tribute to her, was the greeting of her cousin Elizabeth: "Blessed is she who trusted that God's words to her would be fulfilled" (Lk. 1:45). For it was that continual trust in the providence of God which most characterized her faith.

All her earthly life was a "pilgrimage of faith" (cf. *Lumen gentium*, 58). For like us she walked in shadows and hoped for things unseen. She knew the contradictions of our earthly life. She was promised

that her Son would be given David's throne, but at His birth, there was no room even at the inn. Mary still believed. The angel said her child would be called the Son of God; but she would see Him slandered, betrayed and condemned, and left to die as a thief on the cross. Even yet, Mary "trusted that God's words to her would be fulfilled" (Lk. 1:45) and that "nothing was impossible with God" (Lk. 1:37).

This woman of faith, Mary of Nazareth, the Mother of God, has been given to us as a model in our pilgrimage of faith. From Mary we learn to surrender to God's will in all things. From Mary, we learn to trust even when all hope seems gone. From Mary, we learn to love Christ, her Son and the Son of God. For Mary is not only the Mother of God, she is Mother of the Church as well. In every stage of the march through history, the Church has benefited from the prayer and protection of the Virgin Mary. Holy Scripture and the experience of the faithful see the Mother of God as the one who in a very special way is united with the Church at the most difficult moments in her history, when attacks on the Church became most threatening. Precisely in periods when Christ, and therefore His Church, provokes deliberated contradiction, Mary appears particularly close to the Church, because for her the Church is always her beloved Christ.

I therefore exhort you in Christ Jesus, to continue to look to Mary as the model of the Church, as the best example of the discipleship of Christ. Learn from her to be always faithful, to trust that God's Word to you will be fulfilled, and that nothing is impossible with God. Turn to Mary frequently in your prayer "for never was it known that anyone who fled to her protection, implored her help or sought her intercession was left unaided.''

As a great sign that has appeared in the heavens, Mary guides and sustains us on our pilgrim way, urging us on to ''the victory that overcomes the world, our faith'' (1 Jn. 5:5).

HOLY FATHER PRAISES AND BLESSES AMERICA

On October 6, Pope John Paul went to the White House for an historic meeting with the President of the United States, Mr. Jimmy Carter. Present for the occasion were Mrs. Carter and daughter Amy, and about 3,000 invited guests including members of Congress, the Supreme Court, the Cabinet and the White House staff, who met on the north lawn.

After a brief welcome address by the President, the Holy Father spoke as follows:

Mr. President,

I wish to express my most sincere thanks for your kind words of welcome to the White House. It is indeed a great honor for me to meet with the President of the United States during a visit of which the aims are spiritual and religious in nature. May I convey at the same time to you, and through you to all your fellow Americans, my profound respect for all the federal and state authorities of this nation and for its beloved people. In the course of the last few days, I have had the opportunity to see some of your cities and rural areas. My only regret is that the time is too short to bring my greetings personally to all parts of this country, but I want to assure you that my esteem and affection go out to every man, woman and child without distinction.

Divine Providence in its own designs has called me from my native Poland to be the successor of Peter in the See of Rome and the leader of the Catholic Church. It gives me great joy to be the first Pope in history to come to the Capital of this nation, and I thank Almighty God for this blessing.

In accepting your courteous invitation, Mr. President, I have also hoped that our meeting today would serve the cause of world peace, international understanding and the promotion of full respect for human rights everywhere.

Mr. Speaker and honorable members of Congress, distinguished members of the cabinet and of the judiciary, ladies and gentlemen,

Your presence here honors me greatly and I deeply appreciate the expression of respect which you thus extend to me. My gratitude goes to each one of you personally for your kind welcome, and to all I wish to say how profoundly I esteem your mission as stewards of the common good of all the people of America.

I come from a nation with a long tradition of deep Christian faith and with a national history marked by many upheavals; for more than a hundred years Poland was even erased from the political map of Europe. But it is also a country marked by a deep veneration for those values without which no society can prosper: love of freedom, cultural creativity, and the conviction that common endeavors for the good of society must be guided by a true moral sense. My own spiritual and religious mission impels me to be the messenger of peace and brotherhood, and to witness to the true greatness of every human person. This greatness derives from the love of God, who created us in His own likeness and gave us an eternal destiny. It is in this dignity of the human person that I see the meaning of history, and that I find the principle that gives sense to the role which every human being has to assume for his or her own advancement and for the well-being of the society to which he or she belongs. It is with these sentiments that I greet in you the whole American people, a people that bases its concept of life on spiritual and moral values, on a deep religious sense, on respect for duty and on generosity in the service of humanity—noble traits which are embodied in a particular way in the nation's Capital, with its monuments dedicated to such outstanding national figures as George Washington, Abraham Lincoln and Thomas Jefferson.

I greet the American people in their elected representatives, all of you who serve in Congress to chart, through legislation, the path that will lead every citizen of this country towards the fullest development of his or her potential, and the nation as a whole towards assuming its share of the responsibility for building a world of true freedom and justice. I greet America in all who are vested with authority, which can only be seen as an opportunity for serving your fellow-citizens in the overall development of their true humanity and in the full and unimpeded enjoyment of all their fundamental rights. I salute the people of this land also in the members of the judiciary, who are servants of humanity in the application of justice, and who thus hold in their hands the awesome power of profoundly affecting, by their decisions, the lives of every individual.

For all of you I pray to Almighty God that He may grant you the gift of wisdom in your decisions, prudence in your words and actions, and compassion in the exercise of the authority that is yours, so that in your noble office you will always render true service to the people.

God bless America!

LOVE GOODNESS
AND WALK HUMBLY
WITH YOUR GOD

On October 6, after a private meeting in the President's Oval Office, the two dignitaries came to the south lawn where they addressed another crowd of about 6,000 guests. The Holy Father spoke as follows:

Mr. President,

I am honored to have had, at your kind invitation, the opportunity for a meeting with you; for by your office as President of the United States of America you represent before the world the whole American nation and you hold the immense responsibility of leading this nation in the path of justice and peace. I thank you publicly for this meeting and I thank all those who have contributed to its success. I wish also to reiterate here my deep gratitude for the warm welcome and the many kindnesses which I have received from the American people on my pastoral journey through your beautiful land.

Mr. President,

In responding to the kind words which you have addressed to me, I take the liberty of beginning with the passage from the prophet Micah that you quoted at your inauguration: "You have been told, O man, what is good, and what the Lord requires of you: only to do right and to love goodness, and to walk humbly with your God" (Mi. 6:8). In recalling these words, I

wish to greet you and all the authorities in the individual states and in the nation who are committed to the good of the citizens. There is indeed no other way to put oneself at the service of the whole human person except by seeking the good of every man and woman in all their commitments and activities. Authority in the political community is based on the objective ethical principle that the basic duty of power is the solicitude of the common good of society and that it serves the inviolable rights of the human person. The individuals, families, and various groups which compose the civic community are aware that by themselves they are unable to realize their human potential to the full, and therefore they recognize in a wider community the necessary condition for the ever better attainment of the common good.

I wish to commend those in public authority and all the people of the United States for having given, from the very beginning of the existence of the nation, a special place to some of the most important concerns of the common good. Three years ago, during the bicentennial celebration, which I was fortunate to participate in as the Archbishop of Krakow, it was obvious to every one that concern for what is human and spiritual is one of the basic principles governing the life of this community. It is superfluous to add that respect for the freedom and the dignity of every individual, whatever his origin, race, sex or creed, has been a cherished tenet of the civil creed of America, and that it has been backed up by courageous decisions and actions.

Mr. President, ladies and gentlemen, I know and appreciate this country's efforts for arms limitation, especially of nuclear weapons. Everyone is aware of the terrible risk that the stockpiling of such weapons brings upon humanity. Since it is one of the greatest nations on earth, the United States plays a particularly important part in the quest for greater security in the world and for closer international collaboration. With all my heart I hope that there will be no relaxing of its efforts both to reduce the risk of a fatal and disastrous worldwide conflagration, and to secure a prudent and progressive reduction of the destructive capacity of military arsenals. At the same time, by reason of its special position, may the United States succeed in influencing the other nations to join in a continuing commitment for disarmament. Without wholeheartedly accepting such a commitment how can any nation effectively serve humanity, whose deepest desire is true peace?

Attachment to human values and to ethical concerns, which have been a hallmark of the American people, must be situated, especially in the present context of the growing interdependence of peoples across the globe, within the framework of the view that the common good of society embraces not just the individual nation to which one belongs but the citizens of the whole world. I would encourage every action for the reinforcement of peace in the world, a peace based on liberty and justice, on charity and truth. The present-day relationships between peoples and between nations demand the establishment of greater international cooperation also in the economic field. The more powerful a nation is, the greater becomes its international responsibility, the greater also must be its commitment to the betterment of the lot of those whose very humanity is constantly being threatened by want and need. It is my fervent hope that all the powerful nations in the world will deepen their awareness of the principle of human solidarity within the one great human family. America, which in the past decades has demonstrated goodness and generosity in providing food for the hungry of the world, will, I am sure, be able to match this generosity with an equally convincing contribution to the establishing of a world order that will create the necessary economic and trade conditions for a more just relationship between all the nations of the world, in respect for their dignity and their own personality. Since people are suffering under international inequality, there can be no question of giving up the pursuit of international solidarity, even if it involves a notable change in the attitudes and life-styles of those blessed with a larger share of the world's goods.

Mr. President, ladies and gentlemen, in touching upon the comon good, which embodies the aspiration of all human beings to the full development of their capacities and the proper protection of their rights, I have dealt with areas where the Church that I represent and the political community that is the state share a common concern: the safeguarding of the dignity of the human person, and the search for justice and peace. In their own proper spheres, the political community and the Church are mutually independent and self-governing. Yet, by a different title, each serves the personal and social vocation of the same human beings.

For her part, the Catholic Church will continue her efforts to cooperate in promoting justice, peace and dignity through the commitment of her leaders and the members of her communities, and through her incessant proclamation that all human beings are created to the image and likeness of God, and that they are brothers and sisters, children of one heavenly Father.

May Almighty God bless and sustain America in her quest for the fullness of liberty, justice and peace.

At the close of his speech the Pope stepped back from the microphone amid a standing ovation and began walking to the side of the platform, chatting cordially with President Carter. Suddenly the Pope returned to the microphone and announced, "The Pope will bless you with the permission of the President of the United States." He then pronounced the traditional papal blessing in Latin over the crowd

APPEALS FOR DISARMAMENT AND END OF ARMS RACE

On October 6, Pope John Paul visited the headquarters of the Organization of American States, was welcomed by the Secretary General, Mr. Orfila, and gave the following address in Spanish to the 26 member nations.

Mr. President, Mr. Secretary General, ladies and gentlemen,

1. It is indeed a pleasure for me to have this opportunity to greet all the distinguished representatives of the different member nations of the Organization of American States. My sincere gratitude goes to you, Mr. President, for the cordial words of welcome you have extended to me. I thank also the Secretary General for his thoughtful invitation to come and visit the headquarters of the oldest of the regional international organizations. It is fitting that, after my visit to the United Nations Organization, the Organization of American States should be the first one among the many intergovernmental organizations and agencies to which I am privileged to address a message of peace and friendship.

The Holy See follows with great interest, and may I say, with special attention, the events and developments that touch upon the well-being of the peoples of the Americas. It felt, therefore, greatly honored by the invitation to send its own permanent observer to this institution—an invitation extended last year by a unanimous decision of the General Assembly. The Holy See sees in regional organizations such as yours intermediary structures that promote a greater internal diversity and vitality in a given area within the global community of nations. The fact that the American continent is provided with an organization concerned with ensuring more continuity for the dialogue between governments, with promoting peace, with advancing full development in solidarity, and with protecting man, his dignity, and his rights, is a factor contributing to the health of the whole human family. The Gospel and Christianity have entered deeply into your history and your cultures. I would like to call on this common tradition in order to present to you some reflections, in full respect for your personal convictions and your own competence, in order to bring to your endeavors an original contribution in a spirit of service.

2. Peace is a most precious blessing that you seek to preserve for your peoples. You are in agreement with me that it is not by accumulating arms that this peace can be ensured in a stable way. Apart from the fact that such accumulation increases in practice the danger of having recourse to arms to settle the disputes that may arise, it takes away considerable material and human resources from the great peaceful tasks of development that are so urgent. It can also tempt some to think that the order built on arms is sufficient to ensure internal peace in the single countries.

I solemnly call on you to do everything in your power to restrain the arms race on this continent.

There are no differences between your countries that cannot be peacefully overcome. What a relief it would be to your peoples, what new opportunities it would provide for their economic, social and cultural progress, and how contagious an example it would give the world, if the difficult enterprise of disarmament were here to find a realistic and resolute solution!

3. The painful experience of the history of my own country, Poland, has shown me how important national sovereignty is when it is served by a state worthy of the name and free in its decisions; how important it is for the protection not only of a people's legitimate material interests, but also of its culture and its soul. Your organization is an organization of states, founded on respect for the full national sovereignty of each, on equal participation in common tasks, and on solidarity between your peoples. The legitimate demand by the states to participate on a basis of equality in the organization's common decisions must be matched by the will to promote within each country an ever more effective participation by the citizens in the responsibility and decisions of the nation through ways that take into account particular traditions, difficulties and historical experiences.

4. However, while such difficulties and experiences can at times call for exceptional measures and a certain period of maturation in preparation for new advances in shared responsibility, they never, never justify any attack on the inviolable dignity of the human person and on the authentic rights that protect this dignity. If certain ideologies and certain ways of interpreting legitimate concern for national security were to result in subjugating to the state man

and his rights and dignity, they would to that extent cease to be human and would be unable to claim without gross deception any Christian reference. In the Church's thinking it is a fundamental principle that social organization is at the service of man, not vice versa. That holds good also for the highest levels of society, where the power of coercion is wielded and where abuses, when they occur, are particularly serious. Besides, a security in which the peoples no longer feel involved, because it no longer protects them in their very humanity, is only a sham. As it grows more and more rigid, it will show symptoms of increasing weakness and rapidly approaching ruin.

Without undue interference, your organization can, by the spirit with which it tackles all the problems in its competence, do much throughout the continent to advance a concept of the state and its sovereignty that is truly human, and that is therefore the basis for the legitimacy of the states and of their acknowledged prerogatives for the service of man.

5. Man! Man is the decisive criterion that dictates and directs all your undertakings, the living value for whose service new initiatives are unceasingly demanded. The words that are most filled with meaning for man—words such as justice, peace, development, solidarity, human rights—are sometimes belittled as a result of systematic suspicion or party and sectarian ideological censure. They then lose their power to mobilize and attract. They will recover it only if respect for the human person and commitment to the human person are explicitly brought back to the center of all considerations. When we speak of the right to life, to physical and moral integrity, to nourishment, to housing, to education, to health care, to

employment, to shared responsibility in the life of the nation, we speak of the human person. It is this human person whom faith makes us recognize as created in the image of God and destined for an eternal goal. It is this human person that is often threatened and hungry, without decent housing and employment, without access to the cultural heritage of his or her people or of humanity, and without a voice to make his or her distress heard. The great cause of full development in solidarity must be given new life by those who in one degree or another enjoy these blessings, for the service of all those—and there are many of them still on your continent—who are deprived of them to a sometimes dramatic extent.

6. The challenge of development deserves your full attention. In this field, too, what you achieve can be an example for humanity. The problems of rural and urban areas, of industry and agriculture, and of the environment are to a large extent a common task. The energetic pursuit of these will help to spread throughout the continent a sentiment of universal fraternity that extends beyond borders and regimes. Without any disregard for the responsibilities of sovereign states, you discover that it is a logical requirement for you to deal with problems, such as unemployment, migration and trade, as common concerns whose continental dimension increasingly demands more organic solutions on a continental scale. All that you do for the human person will halt violence and the threats of subversion and destabilization. For, by accepting courageous revisions demanded by "this single fundamental point of view, namely, the welfare of man—or, let us say, of the person in the community—which must, as a fundamental

factor in the common good, constitute the essential criterion for all programs, systems and regimes'' (*Redemptor hominis,* 17), you direct the energies of your peoples towards the peaceful satisfaction of their aspirations.

7. The Holy See will always be happy to make its own disinterested contribution to this work. The local churches in the Americas will do the same within the framework of their various responsibilities. By advancing the human person and his or her dignity and rights, they serve the earthly city, its cohesion and its lawful authorities. The full religious freedom that they ask for is in order to serve, not in order to oppose the legitimate autonomy of civil society and of its own means of action. The more all citizens are able to exercise habitually their freedoms in the life of the nation, the more readily will the Christian communities be able to dedicate themselves to the central task of evangelization, namely, the preaching of the Gospel of Jesus Christ, the source of life, strength, justice and peace.

(English)

With fervent prayers for prosperity and concord, I invoke upon this important assembly, upon the representatives of all the member states and their families, upon all the beloved peoples of the Americas, the choicest favors and blessings of Almighty God.

(French)

My visit here, in the Hall of the Americas, before this noble assembly dedicated to inter-American collaboration, expresses at the same time a wish and a prayer. My wish is that, in all the nations of this continent, no man, woman or child may ever feel abandoned by the constituted authorities, to whom they are ready to accord their full confidence to the extent that those authorities seek the good of all. My prayer is that Almighty God may grant His light to the peoples and the governments, that they may always discover new means of collaboration for building up a fraternal and just society.

[Portuguese]

One last word before I leave you—with great regret—after this first brief visit to your esteemed organization. When I visited Mexico, at the beginning of the year, I was amazed at the enthusiasm, spontaneity and joy of living of its people. I am convinced that you will succeed in preserving the rich human and cultural heritage of all your peoples, and thus maintain the indispensable basis for true progress, which is constituted, always and everywhere, by respect for the supreme dignity of man.

IT IS GOD WHO GIVES MEANING TO OUR LIVES

After the Pope's visit and address to the Organization of American States, on October 6, the Holy Father greeted a large concourse of people who had gathered outside the building. He spoke to them in English and in Spanish as follows:

Dear friends,

Thank you for coming here to greet me. To all of you: peace and joy!

Every time I have the opportunity to meet with a group of people, it gives me great happiness, for in you I see my brothers and sisters, children of the same God, who is our Father, and who has created us with a unique beauty and richness: the great beauty of being free human beings, capable of knowing truth, of offering love and understanding to each other, and of joining hands to make the world a better place to live in.

I have met many people during the last few days, many different people: in Ireland, at the United Nations, in the cities and rural areas of America, at this great Organization of American States. I have enjoyed being with them, but above all I have rejoiced in seeing how strongly every one believes in the possibility of bringing peace and well-being to all men, women and children in the world. So, I would like to encourage you also in your dedication to truth and to justice, without which real peace can never exist.

One of the temptations of the modern world is a growing materialism in the outlook of people and of society itself. Many people have been deceived in this regard; they have been led to think that money, pleasure, comfort or self-indulgence can be substitutes for spiritual values.

So, I invite all of you not to lose sight of the things that really matter, the things of the spirit; and let us remember, above all, that it is God who gives meaning to our lives.

To all of you, young and old, I say: do not let the material things of life rob you of the things that really count: God's love for you, and your love for one another.

God bless you!

The Holy Father then spoke in Spanish to the group.

Beloved Spanish-speaking friends,

I have just visited the headquarters of the Organization of American States, where I met the representatives of this geographical area, to whom I brought a message of peace, friendship, encouragement and collaboration on the part of the Church.

The Pope's interest in this international regional Organization is intended to signify also an interest in each of your countries and an interest in each one of you, as family groups or as persons.

I now extend to you with all cordiality the greeting I addressed to the representatives of the American States. I likewise ask God that you may always be able to look to this Organization with eyes of hope and as a place in which your legitimate expectations find an echo, directed towards aims of greater human and Christian dignity.

Throughout my journey in the United States, I am well aware that, scattered among the large crowds and cities, I am also meeting numerous groups of the Spanish community. Let no one feel forgotten by the Pope, but respected and loved in his dignity as a man, with his own cultural and personal values, and as a Christian and son of God as well.

I exhort you, your friends and all Spaniards to sentiments of solidarity, and I encourage you to keep your human and Christian values with courage and constancy.

Receive, all of you, finally, my friendly regards and my affectionate blessing.

DIPLOMACY: THE ART OF MAKING PEACE

On Saturday evening, October 6, John Paul II received the Diplomatic Corps in the Apostolic Delegation at Washington, and addressed them as follows:

Your Excellencies,
Ladies and Gentlemen,

In the course of this visit, so agreeable and so demanding at the same time, I am particularly happy at this opportunity which is given to me this evening to meet the members of the Diplomatic Corps in mission at Washington.

Your presence here honors me. It is an honor not only to my person but to the head of the Catholic Church, and I thank you very cordially for it. I also see in this act of courtesy an encouragement for the activity of the Catholic Church and of the Holy See in the service of mankind.

This concern with the service of mankind is common to the Diplomatic Corps and to the Holy See: each acts in its own field, pursuing its own mission perseveringly, but they are both united by the great cause of understanding and solidarity among peoples and nations.

SUPREME VALUES

Yours is a noble task. In spite of the inevitable difficulties, setbacks and failures, diplomacy draws its importance from the fact that it is one of the ways to be traversed when seeking out the peace and progress of the whole of mankind. "Diplomacy," my predecessor, Paul VI, said, "is the art of making peace" (Address to the Diplomatic Corps, Rome, January 12, 1974). The efforts of diplomats to establish or maintain peace, whether at a bilateral or multilateral level, are not always crowned with success. It is necessary, however, to encourage them always, today as in the past, so as to bring forth new initiatives, map out new paths, with the patience and tenacity which are the diplomat's eminent qualities. Since I am speaking in the name of Christ, who proclaimed that He was "the way, the truth and the life" (Jn. 14:6), I would like also to draw attention to other qualities which seem to me indispensable if it is desired that at the present time diplomacy should meet the hopes set in it. The supreme values, both moral and spiritual, must, in fact, be more and more deeply integrated in the aims pursued by peoples and in the means used to reach them.

FIRST REQUIREMENT

Truth is the first of these moral requirements which must prevail in relations among nations and peoples. For the thirteenth World Day of Peace (January 1, 1980), I have chosen as the theme: "Truth, the power of peace." I am convinced that the governments and nations that you represent will join once more, as they have done so admirably in the past, in this great enterprise: to instill truth into all relations, whether they be political or economic, bilateral or multilateral.

Now, too often, falsehood exists in our life, at the personal as well as the collective level, bringing with it suspicion where truth is indispensable; then dialogue becomes difficult, which makes all collaboration or understanding nearly impossible. To put truth in all relations is to work at peace, for that makes it possible to find solutions for world problems that are in conformity with reason and justice, in conformity, in a word, with the truth about man.

PEACE MUST BE HUMAN

That brings me to the second point I would like to bring up. For peace to be real and lasting, it must be *human.* The desire for peace is universal. It dwells in the heart of every human being and it cannot be satisfied unless the human person is placed at the center of all efforts to bring forth unity and brotherhood among nations.

Your mission as diplomats is based on the mandate you have received from those who are responsible for the well-being of your nations. This power in which you share cannot be separated from the objective requirements of the moral order and the destiny of every human being. I take the liberty of telling you again here what I declared in my first encyclical letter: "The fundamental duty of power is solicitude for the common good of society; this is what gives power its fundamental rights. Precisely in the name of these premises of the objective ethical order, the rights of power can only be understood on the basis of respect for the objective and inviolable rights of man. The common good that authority in the State serves is brought to full realization only when all the citizens are sure of their rights. The lack of this leads to the dissolution of society, opposition by citizens to authority, or a situation of oppression, intimidation, violence, and terrorism, of which many examples have been provided by the totalitarianisms of this century. Thus the principle of human rights is of profound concern to the area of social justice and is the measure by which it can be tested in the life of political bodies'' *(Redemptor hominis,* 17).

TRUTH ABOUT MAN

These reflections take on all their importance also in the field that concerns you directly, the pursuit of international peace, of justice among nations and of the cooperation of all peoples in solidarity. In the final analysis, the success of diplomacy today will be in the victory of the truth about man.

I invoke the blessings of almighty God on your mission, which entails the double requirement of defending the interests of your countries, while putting them in the context of universal peace; on yourselves, who are peacemakers; on your partners and your families, who sustain you and encourage you; and finally on all those who rely on your devoted service in order that their own dignity as human persons may be recognized and respected. May the peace of God always dwell in your hearts!

GOD WILL UNVEIL
THE TRUE GREATNESS
OF YOURSELVES

On the Catholic University campus outside the Shrine of the Immaculate Conception, a large group of students awaited the arrival of Pope John Paul on Sunday morning, October 7. Some had spent the night in the open in the hope of getting better places. To the enthusiastic group the Holy Father delivered the following address.

Dear students of the Catholic University,

My first greeting on arriving at this campus is for you! To all of you I offer the peace and joy of our Lord Jesus Christ! I am told that you have held an all-night prayer vigil to ask God's blessing on my visit. Thank you most cordially for such a wonderful expression of communion with me, and for such a beautiful gift. I would like to talk to you at length; I would like to listen to you and know what you think about yourselves and the world. But the time I have been given is so short.

One thing you have told me already: by choosing to welcome me with the offering of your prayers, you have demonstrated that you understand what is most important in your lives—your contact with God, your searching for the meaning of life by listening to Christ as He speaks to you in the Scriptures. I am pleased to know that reflection on spiritual and religious values is part of your desire to live fully this time of your lives. Materialistic concerns and one-sided values are never sufficient to fill the heart and mind of a human person. A life reduced to the sole dimension of possessions, of consumer goods, of temporal concerns will never let you discover and enjoy the full richness of your humanity. It is only in God—in Jesus, God-made-man—that you will fully understand what you are. He will unveil to you the true greatness of yourselves: that you are redeemed by Him and taken up in His love; that you are made truly free in Him who said about Himself: "If the son frees you, you will be free indeed" (Jn. 8:36).

I know that you, like students all over the world, are troubled by the problems that weigh on society around you and on the whole world. Look at those problems, explore them, study them and accept them as a challenge. But do it in the light of Christ. He is "the way, and the truth, and the life" (Jn. 14:6). He put all human life in the true dimension of truth and of authentic love. True knowledge and true freedom are in Jesus. Make Jesus always part of your hunger for truth and justice, and part of your dedication to the well-being of your fellow human beings.

Enjoy the privileges of your youth: the right to be dynamic, creative and spontaneous; the right to be full of hope and joy; the opportunity to explore the marvellous world of science and knowledge; and above all the chance to give of yourself to others in generous and joyful service.

I leave you now with this prayer: that the Lord Jesus will reveal Himself to each one of you, that He will give you the strength to go out and profess that you are Christian, that He will show you that He alone can fill your hearts. Accept His freedom and embrace His truth, and be messengers of the certainty that you have been truly liberated through the death

and resurrection of the Lord Jesus. This will be the new experience, the powerful experience, that will generate, through you, a more just society and a better world.

God bless you and may the joy of Jesus be always with you!

Arturo Mari

We can convincingly proclaim ''the unsearchable riches of Christ'' (Eph. 3:8) only if we maintain fidelity to the love and friendship of Jesus, only if we continue to live in the faith of the Son of God.

Arturo Mari

The mission of evangelization that is mine and yours, must be carried out through a constant unselfish witnessing to the unity of love. Love is the force that opens hearts to the word of Jesus and to His redemption.

Arturo Mari

We who, by divine mandate, must proclaim the duties of the Christian law, and who must call our people to constant conversion and renewal, know that Saint Paul's invitation applies above all to ourselves: ''You must put on the new man created in God's image, whose justice and holiness are born of truth'' (Eph. 4:24).

When I lift up my eyes, I see in you the People of God, united to sing the praises of the Lord and to celebrate His Eucharist.

Because of my personal pastoral responsibility, and because of our common pastoral reponsibility for the People of God in the United States, I desire to strengthen you in your ministry of faith as local pastors, and to support you in your individual and joint pastoral activities by encouraging you to stand fast in the holiness and truth of our Lord Jesus Christ.

Uniphoto/CMS

I pray to Almighty God that He may grant you the gift of wisdom in your decisions, prudence in your words and actions, and compassion in the exercise of the authority that is yours, so that in your noble office you will always render true service to the people. God bless America!

My own spiritual and religious mission impels me to be the messenger of peace and brotherhood, and to witness to the true greatness of every human person. This greatness derives from the love of God, who created us in His own likeness and gave us an eternal destiny.

One thing you have told me already: by choosing to welcome me with the offering of your prayers, you have demonstrated that you understand what is most important in your lives—your contact with God, your searching for the meaning of life by listening to Christ as He speaks to you in the Scriptures.

I leave you now with this prayer: that the Lord Jesus will reveal Himself to each one of you, that He will give you the strength to go out and profess that you are Christian, that He will show you that He alone can fill your hearts.

Arturo Mari

As daughters of the Church—a title cherished by so many of your great saints—you are called to a generous and loving adherence to the authentic Magisterium of the Church, which is a solid guarantee of the fruitfulness of all your apostolates and an indispensable condition for the proper interpretation of the ''signs of the times.''

A mother of thirteen children and a pro-life advocate, Mrs. Alexander Thomas receives Holy Communion from the Pope. The Thomas family are personal friends of the Holy Father.

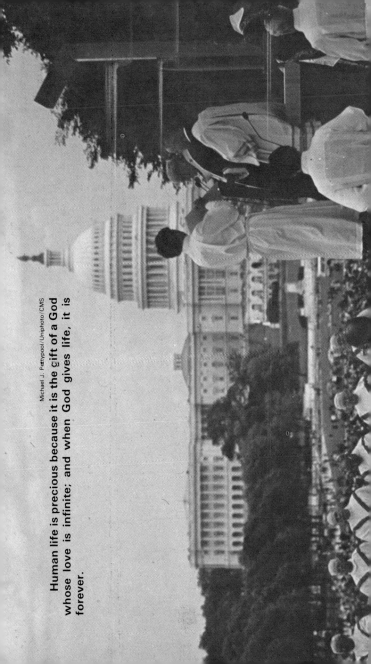

Human life is precious because it is the gift of a God whose love is infinite; and when God gives life, it is forever.

Michael J. Pettypool/Uniphoto/CMS

We are confident that Mary, the Mother of God and the Mother of life, will give us her help so that our way of living will always reflect our admiration and gratitude for God's gift of love that is life.

Today, therefore, my final prayer is this: that God may bless America, so that she may increasingly become—and truly be—and long remain—"One nation, *under God,* indivisible. With liberty and justice for all."

MARY, SIGN OF HOPE FOR ALL GENERATIONS

In the Church of the Immaculate Conception at the National Shrine, Pope John Paul addressed the large gathering of religious women on the morning of October 7. After listening to an address of welcome by one of the sisters, the Holy Father invited the religious to look on Mary as their model. He spoke as follows:

My first desire, in this National Shrine of the Immaculate Conception, is to direct my thoughts, to turn my heart to the woman of salvation history. In the eternal design of God, this woman, Mary, was chosen to enter into the work of the Incarnation and Redemption. This design of God was to be actuated through her free decision given in obedience to the divine will. Through her "yes," a "yes" that pervades and is reflected in all history, she consented to be the Virgin Mother of our saving God, the handmaid of the Lord, and at the same time, the Mother of all the faithful who in the course of the centuries would become brothers and sisters of her Son. Through her, the Sun of justice was to rise in the world. Through her the great Healer of humanity, the reconciler of hearts and consciences, her Son, the God-Man, Jesus Christ, was to transform the human condition and by His death and resurrection uplift the entire human family. As a great sign that appeared in the heavens, in the fullness of time, the woman dominates all history as the Virgin Mother of the Son and as the Spouse of the Holy Spirit, as the handmaid of humanity.

The woman becomes also, by association with her Son, the sign of contradiction to the world, and at the same time the sign of hope, whom all generations shall call blessed. The woman who conceived spiritually before she conceived physically, the woman who accepted the Word of God, the woman who was inserted intimately and irrevocably into the mystery of the Church, exercising a spiritual motherhood with regard to all peoples. The woman who is honored as Queen of Apostles, without herself being inserted into the hierarchical constitution of the Church, and yet this woman made all hierarchy possible because she gave to the world the Shepherd and Bishop of our souls. This woman, this Mary of the Gospels, who is not mentioned as being at the Last Supper, comes back again at the foot of the cross, in order to consummate her contribution to salvation history. By her courageous act she prefigures and anticipates the courage of all women throughout the ages who concur in bringing forth Christ in every generation.

At Pentecost, the Virgin Mother once again comes forward to exercise her role in union with the apostles, with and in and over the Church. Yet again, she conceived of the Holy Spirit to bring forth Jesus in the fullness of His Body, the Church, never to leave Him, never to abandon Him, but to continue to love and to cherish Him through the ages.

This is the woman of history and destiny who inspires us today, the woman who speaks to us of femininity, human dignity and love, and who is the greatest expression of total consecration to Jesus Christ, in whose name we are gathered today.

WITHOUT LOVE RELIGIOUS LIFE IS INCOMPREHENSIBLE

After his words upholding the dignity of the Blessed Virgin as model for religious, the Holy Father spoke to all the religious gathered in the Shrine of the Immaculate Conception, lauding their invaluable contribution to the life of the Church. He spoke as follows:

Dear Sisters,

May the grace, love and peace of God our Father and our Lord Jesus Christ be with you.

I welcome this opportunity to speak with you today. I am happy for this occasion because of my esteem for religious life, and my gratitude to women religious for their invaluable contribution to the mission and very life of the Church.

I am especially pleased that we are gathered here in the National Shrine of the Immaculate Conception, for the Virgin Mary is the model of the Church, the Mother of the faithful and the perfect example of consecrated life.

1. On the day of our Baptism, we received the greatest gift God can bestow on any man or woman. No other honor, no other distinction will equal its value. For we were freed from sin and incorporated into Christ Jesus and His Body, the Church. That day and every day after, we were chosen ''to live through love in his presence'' (Eph. 1:4).

In the years that followed our Baptism, we grew in awareness—even wonder—of the mystery of Christ. By listening to the beatitudes, by meditating on the cross, conversing with Christ in prayer and receiving Him in the Eucharist, we progressed toward the day, that particular moment of our life, when we solemnly ratified with full awareness and freedom our Baptismal consecration. We affirmed our determination to live always in union with Christ, and to be, according to the gifts given us by the Holy Spirit, a generous and loving member of the People of God.

2. Your religious consecration builds on this common foundation which all Christians share in the Body of Christ. Desiring to perfect and intensify what God had begun in your life by Baptism, and discerning that God was indeed offering you the gift of the evangelical counsels, you willed to follow Christ more closely, to conform your life more completely to that of Jesus Christ, in and through a distinctive religious community. This is the essence of religious consecration: to profess within and for the benefit of the Church, poverty, chastity and obedience in response to God's special invitation, in order to praise and serve God in greater freedom of heart (cf. 1 Cor. 7:34-35) and to have one's life more closely conformed to Christ in the manner of life chosen by Him and His Blessed Mother (cf. *Perfectae caritatis,* 1; *Lumen gentium,* 46).

3. Religious consecration not only deepens your personal commitment to Christ, but it also strengthens your relationship to His spouse, the Church. Religious consecration is a distinctive manner of living in the Church, a particular way of fulfilling the life of faith and service begun in Baptism.

On her part, the Church assists you in your discernment of God's will. Having accepted and authenticated the charisms of your various institutes, she then unites your religious profession to the celebration of Christ's Paschal Mystery.

You are called by Jesus Himself to verify and manifest in your lives and in your activities your deepened relationship with His Church. This bond of union with the Church must also be shown in the spirit and apostolic endeavors of every religious institute. For faithfulness to Christ, especially in religious life, can never be separated from faithfulness to the Church. This ecclesial dimension of the vocation of religious consecration has many important practical consequences for institutes themselves and for each individual member. It implies, for example, a greater public witness to the Gospel, since you represent, in a special way as women religious, the spousal relationship of the Church to Christ. The ecclesial dimension also requires, on the part of individual members as well as entire institutes, a faithfulness to the original charisms which God has given to His Church, through your founders and foundresses. It means that institutes are called to continue to foster, in dynamic faithfulness, those corporate commitments which were related to the original charism, which were authenticated by the Church, and which still fulfill important needs of the People of God. A good example in this regard would be the Catholic school system which has been invaluable for the Church in the United States, an excellent means not only for communicating the Gospel of Christ to the students, but also for permeating the entire community with Christ's truth and His love. It is one of the apostolates in which women religious have made, and are still making an incomparable contribution.

4. Dear Sisters in Christ: Jesus must always be first in your lives. His person must be at the center of your activities—the activities of every day. No other person and no other activity can take precedence over Him. For your whole life has been consecrated to Him. With St. Paul you have to say: "All I want is to

know Christ and the power of his resurrection and to share his sufferings by reproducing the pattern of his death" (Phil. 3:10).

Christ remains primary in your life only when He enjoys the first place in your mind and heart. Thus you must continuously unite yourself to Him in prayer. Without prayer, religious life has no meaning. It has lost contact with its source, it has emptied itself of substance, and it no longer can fulfill its goal. Without prayer there can be no joy, no hope, no peace. For prayer is what keeps us in touch with Christ. The incisive words written in *Evangelica testificatio* cause us all to reflect: "Do not forget the witness of history: faithfulness to prayer or its abandonment is the test of the vitality or decadence of religious life" *(Evangelica testificatio,* 42).

5. Two dynamic forces are operative in religious life: your love for Jesus—and, in Jesus, for all who belong to Him—and His love for you.

We cannot live without love. If we do not encounter love, if we do not experience it and make it our own, and if we do not participate intimately in it, our life is meaningless. Without love we remain incomprehensible to ourselves (cf. *Redemptor hominis,* 10).

Thus every one of you needs a vibrant relationship of love to the Lord, a profound loving union with Christ, your Spouse, a love like that expressed in the psalm: "God, you are my God whom I seek, for you my flesh pines and my soul thirsts like the earth, parched, lifeless and without water. Thus have I gazed toward you in the sanctuary to see your power and your glory" (Ps. 63:1-2).

Yet far more important than your love for Christ is Christ's love for you. You have been called by Him, made a member of His Body, consecrated in a life of the evangelical counsels and destined by Him to have a share in the mission that Christ has entrusted to the Church: His own mission of salvation. For this reason, you center your life in the Eucharist. In the Eucharist, you celebrate His death and resurrection and receive from Him the Bread of eternal life. And it is in the Eucharist especially that you are united to the one who is the object of all your love. Here, with Him, you find ever greater reasons to love and serve His brothers and sisters. Here, with Him—with Christ —you find greater understanding and compassion for God's people. And here you find the strength to persevere in your commitment to selfless service.

6. Your service in the Church is then an extension of Christ to whom you have dedicated your life. For it is not yourself that you put forward, but Christ Jesus as Lord. Like John the Baptist, you know that for Christ to increase, you must decrease. And so your life must be characterized by a complete availability: a readiness to serve as the needs of the Church require, a readiness to give public witness to the Christ whom you love.

The need for this public witness becomes a constant call to inner conversion, to justice and holiness of life on the part of each religious. It also becomes an invitation to each Institute to reflect on the purity of its corporate ecclesial witness. And it is for this reason that in my address last November to the International Union of Superiors General I mentioned that it is not unimportant that your consecration to God should be manifested in the permanent exterior sign of a simple and suitable religious garb. This is not only my personal conviction, but also the desire of the Church, often expressed by so many of the faithful.

As daughters of the Church—a title cherished by so many of your great saints—you are called to a generous and loving adherence to the authentic Magisterium of the Church, which is a solid guarantee of the fruitfulness of all your apostolates and an indispensable condition for the proper interpretation of the "signs of the times."

7. The contemplative life occupies today and forever a place of great honor in the Church. The prayer of contemplation was found in the life of Jesus Himself, and has been a part of religious life in every age. I take this opportunity therefore—as I did in Rome, in Mexico and in Poland—to encourage again all who are members of contemplative communities. Know that you shall always fulfill an important place in the Church, in her mission of salvation, in her service to the whole community of the People of God. Continue faithfullly, confidently and prayerfully, in the rich tradition that has been handed down to you.

In closing, I remind you, with sentiments of admiration and love, that the aim of religious life is to render praise and glory to the Most Holy Trinity, and, through your consecration, to help humanity enter into fullness of life in the Father, and in the Son and in the Holy Spirit. In all your planning and in all your activities, try also to keep this aim before you. There is no greater service you can give; there is no greater fulfillment you can receive. Dear Sisters: today and forever: Praised be Jesus Christ!

"THANK YOU, MOTHER, FOR THIS PRESENCE OF YOURS"

After his address to the religious, Pope John Paul spoke to all present on devotion to Mary and its significance for the many people who have come here from various countries of the world and built a new society. His address was a prayer to the Mother of God.

This Shrine speaks to us with the voice of all America, with the voice of all the sons and daughters of America, who have come here from the various countries of the Old World. When they came, they brought with them in their hearts the same love for the Mother of God that was a characteristic of their ancestors and of themselves in their native lands. These people, speaking different languages, coming from different backgrounds of history and tradition in their own countries, came together around the heart of a Mother whom they all had in common. While their faith in Christ made all of them aware of being the one People of God, this awareness became all the more vivid through the presence of the Mother in the work of Christ and the Church.

Today, as I thank you, Mother, for this presence of yours in the midst of the men and women of this land—a presence which has lasted two hundred years —giving a new form to their social and civic lives in the United States, I commend them all to your Immaculate Heart.

With gratitude and joy I recall that you have been honored as Patroness of the United States, under the title of your Immaculate Conception since the days of the Sixth Provincial Council of Baltimore in 1846.

I commend to you, Mother of Christ, and I entrust to you the Catholic Church: the Bishops, priests, deacons, individual religious and religious institutes, the seminarians, vocations, and the apostolate of the laity in its various aspects.

In a special way, I entrust to you the well-being of the Christian families of this country, the innocence of children, the future of the young, the vocation of single men and women. I ask you to communicate to all the women of the United States a deep sharing in the joy that you experienced in your closeness to Jesus Christ, your Son. I ask you to preserve all of them in freedom from sin and evil, like the freedom which was yours in a unique way from that moment of supreme liberation in your Immaculate Conception.

I entrust to you the great work of ecumenism here, in this land, in which those who confess Christ belong to different Churches and communions. I do this in order that the words of Christ's prayer may be fulfilled: "That they may be one." I entrust to you the consciences of men and women and the voice of public opinion, in order that they may not be opposed to the law of God but follow it as the fount of truth and good.

I add to this, Mother, the great cause of justice and peace in the modern world, in order that the force and energy of love may prevail over hatred and destructiveness, and in order that the children of light may not lack concern for the welfare of the whole human family.

Mother, I commend and entrust to you all that goes to make up earthly progress, asking that it should not be one-sided, but that it should create conditions for the full spiritual advancement of individuals, families, communities and nations. I commend to you the poor, the suffering, the sick and the handicapped, the aging and the dying. I ask you to reconcile those in sin, to heal those in pain, and to uplift those who have lost their hope and joy. Show to those who struggle in doubt the light of Christ your Son.

Bishops of the Church in the United States have chosen your Immaculate Conception as the mystery to hold the patronage over the People of God in this land. May the hope contained in this mystery overcome sin and be shared by all the sons and daughters of America, and also by the whole human family. At a time when the struggle between good and evil, between the prince of darkness and father of lies and evangelical love is growing more acute, may the light of your Immaculate Conception show to all the way to grace and to salvation. Amen.

A DEEP COMMITMENT TO AUTHENTIC CHRISTIAN LIVING

Pope John Paul II, after entering the university where he met the professors and theologians, addressed them as follows:

Dear brothers and sisters in Christ,

1. Our meeting today gives me great pleasure, and I thank you sincerely for your cordial welcome. My own association with the university world, and more particularly with the Pontifical Theological Faculty of Krakow makes our encounter all the more gratifying for me. I cannot but feel at home with you. The sincere expressions with which the chancellor and the president of the Catholic University of America have confirmed, in the name of all of you, the faithful adherence to Christ and the generous commitment to the service of truth and charity of your Catholic associations and institutions of higher learning are appreciated.

Ninety-one years ago Cardinal Gibbons and the American Bishops requested the foundation of the Catholic University of America, as a university "destined to provide the Church with worthy ministers for the salvation of souls and the propagation of religion and to give the republic most worthy citizens." It seems appropriate to me on this occasion to address myself not only to this great institution, so irrevocably linked to the Bishops of the United States, who have founded it and who generously support it, but also to all the Catholic universities, colleges, and academies of post-secondary learning in your land, those with formal and sometimes juridical links with the Holy See, as well as all those who are "Catholic."

2. Before doing so, though, allow me first to mention the ecclesiastical faculties, three of which are established here at the Catholic University of America. I greet these faculties and all who dedicate their best talents in them. I offer my prayers for the prosperous development and the unfailing fidelity and success of these faculties. In the Apostolic Constitution *Sapientia Christiana,* I have dealt directly with these institutions in order to provide guidance and to ensure that they fulfill their role in meeting the needs of the Christian community in today's rapidly changing circumstances.

I also wish to address a word of praise and admiration for the men and women, especially priests and religious, who dedicate themselves to all forms of campus ministry. Their sacrifices and efforts to bring the true message of Christ to the university world, whether secular or Catholic, cannot go unnoticed.

The Church also greatly appreciates the work and witness of those of her sons and daughters whose vocation places them in non-Catholic universities in your country. I am sure that their Christian hope and Catholic patrimony, bring an enriching and irreplaceable dimension to the world of higher studies.

A special word of gratitude and appreciation also goes to the parents and students who, sometimes at the price of great personal and financial sacrifice, look toward the Catholic universities and colleges for the training that unites faith and science, culture and the Gospel values.

To all engaged in administration, teaching or study in Catholic colleges and universities I would apply the words of Daniel: "They who are learned shall shine like the brightness of the firmament; and those that instruct many in justice, as stars for all eternity" (Dan. 12:3). Sacrifice and generosity have accomplished heroic results in the foundation and development of these institutions. Despite immense financial strain, enrollment problems, and other obstacles, divine Providence and the commitment of the whole People of God have allowed us to see these Catholic institutions flourish and advance.

3. I would repeat here before you what I told the professors and students of the Catholic universities in Mexico when I indicated three aims that are to be pursued. A Catholic university or college must make a specific contribution to the Church and to society through high quality scientific research, in-depth study of problems, and a just sense of history, together with the concern to show the full meaning of the human person regenerated in Christ, thus favoring the complete development of the person. Furthermore, the Catholic university or college must train young men and women of outstanding knowledge who, having made a personal synthesis between faith and culture, will be both capable and willing to assume tasks in the service of the community and of society in general, and to bear witness to their faith before the world. And finally, to be what it ought to be, a Catholic college or university must set up, among its faculty and students, a real community

which bears witness to a living and operative Christianity, a community where sincere commitment to scientific research and study goes together with a deep commitment to authentic Christian living.

This is your identity. This is your vocation. Every university or college is qualified by a specific mode of being. Yours is the qualification of being Catholic, of affirming God, His revelation and the Catholic Church as the guardian and interpreter of that revelation. The term "Catholic" will never be a mere label, either added or dropped according to the pressures of varying factors.

4. As one who for long years has been a university professor, I will never tire of insisting on the eminent role of the university, which is to instruct but also to be a place of scientific research. In both these fields, its activity is closely related to the deepest and noblest aspiration of the human person: the desire to come to the knowledge of truth. No university can deserve the rightful esteem of the world of learning unless it applies the highest standards of scientific research, constantly updating its methods and working instruments, and unless it excels in seriousness, and therefore, in freedom of investigation. Truth and science are not gratuitous conquests, but the result of a surrender to objectivity and of the exploration of all aspects of nature and man. Whenever man himself becomes the object of investigation, no single method, or combination of methods, can fail to take into account, beyond any purely natural approach, the full nature of man. Because he is bound by the total truth on man, the Christian will, in his research and in his teaching, reject any partial vision of human reality,

but he will let himself be enlightened by his faith in the creation of God and the redemption of Christ.

The relationship to truth explains, therefore, the historical bond between the university and the Church. Because she herself finds her origin and her growth in the words of Christ, which are the liberating truth (cf. Jn. 8:32), the Church has always tried to stand by the institutions that serve, and cannot but serve, the knowledge of truth. The Church can rightfully boast of being in a sense the mother of universities. The names of Bologna, Padua, Prague and Paris shine in the earliest history of intellectual endeavor and human progress. The continuity of the historic tradition in this field has come down to our day.

5. An undiminished dedication to intellectual honesty and academic excellence are seen, in a Catholic university, in the perspective of the Church's mission of evangelization and service. This is why the Church asks these institutions, your institutions, to set out, without equivocation, your Catholic nature. This is what I have desired to emphasize in my Apostolic Constitution *Sapientia Christiana,* where I stated: "Indeed, the Church's mission of spreading the Gospel not only demands that the Good News be preached ever more widely and to ever greater numbers of men and women, but that the very power of the Gospel should permeate thought patterns, standards of judgment, and the norms of behavior; in a word, it is necessary that the whole of human culture be steeped in the Gospel. The cultural atmosphere in which a human being lives has a great influence upon his or her way of thinking and, thus, of acting. Therefore, a division between faith and culture is more than a small impediment to evangelization,

while a culture penetrated with the Christian spirit is an instrument that favors the spreading of the Good News" (*Sapientia Christiana,* I). The goals of Catholic higher education go beyond education for production, professional competence, technological and scientific competence; they aim at the ultimate destiny of the human person, at the full justice and holiness born of truth (cf. Eph. 4:24).

6. If then your universities and colleges are institutionally committed to the Christian message, and if they are part of the Catholic community of evangelization, it follows that they have an essential relationship to the hierarchy of the Church. And here I want to say a special word of gratitude, encouragement and guidance for the theologians. The Church needs her theologians, particularly in this time and age so profoundly marked by deep changes in all areas of life and society. The Bishops of the Church, to whom the Lord has entrusted the keeping of the unity of the faith and the preaching of the message—individual Bishops for their dioceses; and Bishops collegially, with the Successor of Peter for the universal Church —we all need your work, your dedication and the fruits of your reflection. We desire to listen to you, and we are eager to receive the valued assistance of your responsible scholarship.

But true theological scholarship, and by the same token, theological teaching, cannot exist and be fruitful without seeking its inspiration and its source in the Word of God as contained in Sacred Scripture and in the Sacred Tradition of the Church, as interpreted by the authentic magisterium throughout history (cf. *Dei verbum,* 10). True academic freedom must be seen in relation to the finality of the academic enter-

prise, which looks to the total truth of the human person. The theologian's contribution will be enriching for the Church only if it takes into account the proper function of the Bishops and the rights of the faithful. It devolves upon the Bishops of the Church to safeguard the Christian authenticity and unity of faith and moral teaching, in accordance with the injunction of the Apostle Paul: "Proclaim the message and, welcome or unwelcome, insist on it. Refute falsehood, correct error, call to obedience..." (2 Tm. 4:2). It is the right of the faithful not to be troubled by theories and hypotheses that they are not expert in judging, or that are easily simplified or manipulated by public opinion for ends that are alien to the truth. On the day of his death, John Paul I stated: "Among the rights of the faithful, one of the greatest is the right to receive God's Word in all its entirety and purity..." (September 28, 1978). It behooves the theologian to be free, but with the freedom that is openness to the truth and the light that comes from faith and from fidelity to the Church.

In concluding I express to you once more my joy in being with you today. I remain very close to your work and your concerns. May the Holy Spirit guide you. May the intercession of Mary, Seat of Wisdom, sustain you always in your irreplaceable service of humanity and the Church. God bless you.

FAITHFULNESS TO THE SPIRIT DEMANDS INTERIOR CONVERSION AND PRAYER

On Sunday, October 7, Pope John Paul met some five hundred representatives of various Christian Churches in the Notre Dame Chapel of Trinity College. After an introductory address by Cardinal William Baum, Archbishop of Washington, the Holy Father spoke as follows:

Dearly beloved in Christ,

1. I am grateful to the providence of God that permits me, on my visit to the United States of America, to have this meeting with other religious leaders, and to be able to join with you in prayer for the unity of all Christians.

It is indeed fitting that our meeting should occur just a short time before the observance of the fifteenth anniversary of the Second Vatican Council's Decree on Ecumenism, *Unitatis redintegratio.* Since the inception of my pontificate, almost a year ago, I have endeavored to devote myself to the service of Christian unity; for, as I stated in my first encyclical, it is certain ''that in the present historical situation of Christianity and of the world the only possibility we see in fulfilling the Church's universal mission, with regard to ecumenical questions, is that of seeking sincerely, perseveringly, humbly, and also courageously, the ways of drawing closer and of union" (*Redemptor hominis*, 6). On a previous occasion, I said that the problem of division within Christianity is "binding in a special way on the Bishop of the ancient Church of Rome, founded on the preaching and the testimonies of the martyrdom of Sts. Peter and Paul" (General Audience, January 17, 1979). And today I wish to reiterate before you the same conviction.

2. With great satisfaction and joy I welcome the opportunity to embrace you, in the charity of Christ, as beloved Christian brethren and fellow disciples of the Lord Jesus. It is a privilege to be able, in your presence and together with you, to give expression to the testimony of John, that "Jesus Christ is the Son of God" (1 Jn. 4:15), and to proclaim that "there is one Mediator between God and men, the man Christ Jesus" (1 Tm. 2:5).

In the united confession of faith in the divinity of Jesus Christ, we feel great love for each other and great hope for all humanity. We experience immense gratitude to the Father, who has sent His Son to be our Savior, "the expiation for our sins, and not for ours only but for the sins of the whole world" (1 Jn. 2:2).

By divine grace we are united in esteem and love for Sacred Scripture, which we recognize as the inspired Word of God. And it is precisely in this Word of God that we learn how much He wants us to be fully one in Him and in His Father. Jesus prays that His followers may be one "so that the world may believe..." (Jn. 17:21). That the credibility of evangelization should, by God's plan, depend on the unity of His followers is a subject of inexhaustible meditation for all of us.

3. I wish to pay homage here to the many splendid ecumenical initiatives that have been realized in this country through the action of the Holy Spirit. In the last fifteen years there has been a positive response to ecumenism by the Bishops of the United States. Through their committee for ecumenical and inter-religious affairs, they have established a fraternal relationship with other Churches and ecclesial communities—a relationship which, I pray, will continue to deepen in the coming years. Conversations are in progress with our brothers from the East, the Orthodox. Here I wish to note that this relationship has been strong in the United States and that soon a theological dialogue will begin on a worldwide basis in an attempt to resolve those difficulties which hinder full unity. There are also American dialogues with the Anglicans, the Lutherans, the Reformed Churches, the Methodists and the Disciples of Christ —all having a counterpart on the international level. A fraternal exchange exists likewise between the Southern Baptists and American theologians.

My gratitude goes to all who collaborate in the matter of joint theological investigation, the aim of which is always the full evangelical and Christian dimension of truth. It is to be hoped that, through such investigation, persons who are well prepared by a solid grounding in their own traditions will contribute to a deepening of the full historical and doctrinal understanding of the issues.

The particular climate and traditions of the United States have been conducive to joint witness in the defense of the rights of the human person, in the pursuit of goals of social justice and peace, and in questions of public morality. These areas of concern must continue to benefit from creative ecumenical action, as must the fostering of esteem for the sacredness of marriage and the support of healthy family life as a major contribution to the well-being of the nation. In this context, recognition must be given to the deep division which still exists over moral and ethical matters. The moral life and the life of faith are so deeply united that it is impossible to divide them.

4. Much has been accomplished but there is still much to be done. We must go forward, however, with a spirit of hope. Even the very desire for the complete unity in faith—which is lacking between us, and which must be achieved before we can lovingly celebrate the Eucharist together in truth—is itself a gift of the Holy Spirit, for which we offer humble praise to God. We are confident that through our common prayer the Lord Jesus will lead us, at a moment dependent on the sovereign action of His Holy Spirit, to the fullness of ecclesial unity.

Faithfulness to the Holy Spirit calls for interior conversion and fervent prayer. In the words of the Second Vatican Council: "This change of heart and holiness of life, along with public and private prayer for the unity of Christians, should be regarded as the soul of the whole ecumenical movement..." (*Unitatis redintegratio,* 8). It is important that every individual Christian search his or her heart to see what may obstruct the attainment of full union among Christians. And let us all pray that the genuine need for the patience to await God's hour will never occasion complacency in the status quo of division in faith. By divine grace may the need for patience never become a substitute for the definitive and generous response which God asks that there be given to His invitation to perfect unity in Christ.

And so, as we are gathered here to celebrate the love of God that is poured out in our hearts by the Holy Spirit, let us be conscious of the call to show supreme fidelity to the will of Christ. Let us together perseveringly ask the Holy Spirit to remove all divisions from our faith, to give us that perfect unity in truth and love for which Christ prayed, for which Christ died: "to gather together in unity the scattered children of God" (Jn. 11:52).

I offer my respectful greeting of grace and peace to those whom you represent, to each of your respective congregations, to all who long for the coming of "our great God and Savior Jesus Christ" (Ti. 2:13).

SO MANY PERSONS COUNT ON YOU!

Returning to the Apostolic Delegation after the ecumenical meeting at Trinity College, the Holy Father spoke as follows to the journalists who had accompanied him on his apostolic journey.

My dear friends of the communications media,

Here we are together again at the end of another journey—a journey which this time has brought me to Ireland, to the United Nations and to the United States of America. The purpose of this journey was to permit the Pope to exercise his function as a herald of peace, in the name of Christ, who was referred to as the Prince of Peace. This message of peace was announced especially in those places and before those audiences where the problem of war and peace is perceived with particular sensitivity and where there exist the conditions of understanding, of good will and of the means necessary to building peace and cooperation among all nations and among all peoples.

SOURCE OF POWER

The word "peace" is a synthesis. It has many components. I have touched on several of these during this journey, and you have diligently reported on these reflections. You have commented on them; you have interpreted them; you have performed the service of stimulating people to think about how they might contribute to a firmer foundation for peace, for cooperation and for justice among all persons.

Now we find ourselves at the moment of parting, in this capital city of one of the most powerful nations in the world. The power of this country, I believe, comes not only from material wealth but from a richness of spirit.

In fact, the name of this city and of the tall monument which dominates it recalls the spirit of George Washington, the first president of the nation, who—with Thomas Jefferson, for whom an imposing memorial also exists here, and with other enlightened individuals—established this country on a foundation which was not only human but also profoundly religious.

E PLURIBUS UNUM

As a consequence, the Catholic Church has been able to flourish here. The millions of faithful who belong to the Church testify to that fact, as they exercise the rights and duties which flow from their faith with full freedom. The great National Shrine of the Immaculate Conception in this city testifies to that fact. The existence in this capital city of two Catholic universities—Georgetown and the Catholic University of America—testifies to that fact. I have observed that the people of the United States of America proudly and gratefully pledge allegiance to their republic as "one nation under God."

This one nation is made up of many members—members of all races, of all religions, of all conditions of life—so that it is a type of microcosm of the world community and accurately reflects the motto *E Pluri-*

bus Unum. As this country courageously abolished the plague of slavery under the presidency of Abraham Lincoln, may it never stop striving for the effective good of all the inhabitants of this one nation and for that unity which reflects its national motto. For this reason, the United States of America gives to all cause to reflect on a spirit which, if well applied, can bring beneficial results for peace in the world community.

I sincerely hope that all of you have profitted from this journey, and that you have had the opportunity to reflect anew on the values which have come from Christianity to the civilization of this new continent. Most of all, however, we can draw hope for a peaceful world community from the example of persons of all races, of all nationalities, and of all religions living together in peace and unity.

FORM AND INFORM

As we prepare to part, my dear friends, I am consoled by the fact that you will continue to inform and to form world public opinion with a profound consciousness of your responsibility and with the realization that so many persons depend on you.

Finally, I say goodbye to you and to America. I thank you again, and with all my heart I ask God to bless you and your families.

ATTACHMENT
TO THE FAITH
AND APOSTOLIC SEE

After meeting the journalists the Holy Father met a group of Knights of Columbus who had followed him along the various stages of his journey in the United States, undertaking a valuable service of organizing the most important and crowded ceremonies. To these the Holy Father addressed the following words.

Dear Knights of Columbus,

It gives me great pleasure to be with you on the occasion of my pastoral visit to the United States. I thank you most sincerely for the respect and love which you have manifested toward me as Successor of Peter, Bishop of Rome and Pastor of the universal Church.

In the person of the Supreme Knight and the members of the Supreme Board, I greet all the Knights of Columbus: the more than one million, three hundred thousand Catholic laymen all over the world, who display a spirit of profound attachment to their Christian faith and of loyalty to the Apostolic See.

Many times in the past, and again today, you have given expression to your solidarity with the mission of the Pope. I see in your support a further proof—if further proof were ever necessary—of your awareness that the Knights of Columbus highly value their vocation to be part of the evangelization effort of the Church. I am happy to recall here what my revered

predecessor, Paul VI, said about this task in his Apostolic Exhortation *Evangelii nuntiandi,* as he emphasized the specific role of the laity: "Their own field of evangelizing activity is the vast and complicated world of politics, society and economics, but also the world of culture, of the sciences and arts, of international life, of the mass media. It also includes other realities which are open to evangelization, such as human love, the family, the education of children and adolescents, professional work and suffering" (no. 70).

These words of one who never ceased to encourage you clearly indicate the road which your association must travel. I am aware of the many efforts you make to promote the use of mass media for the spreading of the Gospel and for the wider diffusion of my own messages. May the Lord reward you, and through your efforts bring forth abundant fruits of evangelization in the Church. May your dedicated activity in turn help you to realize in yourselves those interior attitudes without which no one can truly evangelize: trust in the power of the Holy Spirit, true holiness of life, deep concern for truth, and an ever increasing love for all God's children.

May the Lord's blessing be upon you, upon your families and upon all the Knights of Columbus.

LET US
CELEBRATE LIFE!

About a million persons were present for the Holy Father's con-celebrated Mass on October 7, held on Capitol Mall, the great stretch of green between the Capitol and the Lincoln Memorial. It was the last religious function before the Pope's departure from the United States. After the Gospel the Pope delivered the following homily.

Dear brothers and sisters in Jesus Christ,

1. In His dialogue with His listeners, Jesus was faced one day with an attempt by some Pharisees to get Him to endorse their current views regarding the nature of marriage. Jesus answered by reaffirming the teaching of Scripture: "At the beginning of creation God made them male and female; for this reason a man shall leave his father and mother and the two shall become one. They are no longer two but one in flesh. Therefore let no man separate what God has joined" (Mk. 10:6-9).

The Gospel according to Mark immediately adds the description of a scene with which we are all familiar. This scene shows Jesus becoming indignant when He noticed how His own disciples tried to prevent the people from bringing their children closer to Him. And so He said: "Let the children come to me and do not hinder them. It is to just such as these that the kingdom of God belongs.... Then he embraced them and blessed them, placing his hands on them" (Mk. 10:14-16). In proposing these readings, today's liturgy invites all of us to reflect on the nature of marriage, on the family, and on the value of life—three themes that are so closely interconnected.

INVIOLABILITY OF HUMAN LIFE

2. I shall all the more gladly lead you in reflecting on the Word of God as proposed by the Church today, because all over the world the Bishops are discussing marriage and family life as they are lived in all dioceses and nations. The Bishops are doing this in preparation for the next World Synod of Bishops, which has as its theme: "The Role of the Christian Family in the Contemporary World." Your own Bishops have designated next year as a year of study, planning and pastoral renewal with regard to the family. For a variety of reasons there is a renewed interest throughout the world in marriage, in family life and in the value of all human life.

This very Sunday marks the beginning of the annual Respect Life program, through which the Church in the United States intends to reiterate its conviction regarding the inviolability of human life in all stages. Let us then, all together, renew our esteem for the value of human life, remembering also that, through Christ, all human life has been redeemed.

HUMAN LIFE IS SACRED

3. I do not hesitate to proclaim before you and before the world that all human life—from the moment of conception and through all subsequent stages —is sacred, because human life is created in the image and likeness of God. Nothing surpasses the greatness or dignity of a human person. Human life is not just

an idea or an abstraction; human life is the concrete reality of a being that lives, that acts, that grows and develops; human life is the concrete reality of a being that is capable of love and of service to humanity.

Let me repeat what I told the people during my recent pilgrimage to my homeland: "If a person's right to life is violated at the moment in which he is first conceived in his mother's womb, an indirect blow is struck also at the whole of the moral order, which serves to ensure the inviolable goods of man. Among those goods, life occupies the first place. The Church defends the right to life, not only in regard to the majesty of the Creator, who is the first Giver of this life, but also in respect of the essential good of the human person" (June 8, 1979).

LIFE IS FOREVER

4. Human life is precious because it is the gift of a God whose love is infinite; and when God gives life, it is forever. Life is also precious because it is the expression and the fruit of love. This is why life should spring up within the setting of marriage, and why marriage and the parents' love for one another should be marked by generosity in self-giving. The great danger for family life, in the midst of any society whose idols are pleasure, comfort and independence, lies in the fact that people close their hearts and become selfish. The fear of making permanent commitments can change the mutual love of husband and wife into two loves of self—two loves existing side by side until they end in separation.

In the sacrament of marriage, a man and a woman —who at Baptism became members of Christ and hence have the duty of manifesting Christ's attitudes in their lives—are assured of the help they need to develop their love in a faithful and indissoluble union, and to respond with generosity to the gift of parenthood. As the Second Vatican Council declared: Through this sacrament, Christ Himself becomes present in the life of the married couple and accompanies them, so that they may love each other and their children, just as Christ loved His Church by giving Himself up for her (cf. *Gaudium et spes,* 48; cf. Eph. 5:25).

FAMILY RESPONSIBILITY

5. In order that Christian marriage may favor the total good and development of the married couple, it must be inspired by the Gospel, and thus be open to new life—new life to be given and accepted generously. The couple is also called to create a family atmosphere in which children can be happy and lead full and worthy human and Christian lives.

To maintain a joyful family requires much from both the parents and the children. Each member of the family has to become, in a special way, the servant of the others and share their burdens (cf. Gal. 6:2; Phil. 2:2). Each one must show concern, not only for his or her own life, but also for the lives of the other members of the family: their needs, their hopes, their ideals. Decisions about the number of children and the sacrifices to be made for them must not be taken only with a view to adding to comfort and preserving a peaceful existence. Reflecting upon this matter before God, with the graces drawn from the sacrament, and guided by the teaching of the Church, parents will remind themselves that it is certainly less serious to deny their children certain comforts or material advantages than to deprive them of the presence of brothers and sisters, who could help them to grow in humanity and to realize the beauty of life at all its ages and in all its variety.

If parents fully realized the demands and the opportunities that this great sacrament brings, they could not fail to join in Mary's hymn to the Author of life—to God who has made them His chosen fellow workers.

EVERY PERSON UNIQUE

6. All human beings ought to value every person for his or her uniqueness as a creature of God, called to be a brother or sister of Christ by reason of the Incarnation and the universal redemption. For us, the sacredness of human life is based on these premises. And it is on these same premises that there is based our celebration of life—all human life. This explains our efforts to defend human life against every influence or action that threatens or weakens it, as well as our endeavors to make every life more human in all its aspects.

And so, we will stand up every time that human life is threatened. When the sacredness of life before birth is attacked, we will stand up and proclaim that no one ever has the authority to destroy unborn life. When a child is described as a burden or is looked upon only as a means to satisfy an emotional need, we will stand up and insist that every child is a unique and unrepeatable gift of God, with the right to a loving and united family. When the institution of marriage is abandoned to human selfishness or reduced to a temporary, conditional arrangement that can easily be terminated, we will stand up and affirm the indissolubility of the marriage bond. When the value of the family is threatened because of social and economic pressures, we will stand up and reaffirm that the family is "necessary not only for the private good of every person, but also for the common good of every society, nation and state" (general audience, January 3, 1979). When freedom is used to dominate the weak, to squander natural resources and energy, and to deny basic necessities to people, we will stand up and reaffirm the demands of justice and social love. When the sick, the aged or the dying are abandoned in loneliness, we will stand up and proclaim that they are worthy of love, care and respect.

UPHOLD VALUES

7. I make my own the words which Paul VI spoke last year to the American Bishops: "We are convinced, moreover, that all efforts made to safeguard human rights actually benefit life itself. Everything aimed at banishing discrimination—in law or in fact—which is based on race, origin, color, culture, sex or religion (cf. *Octogesima adveniens*, 16) is a service to life. When the rights of minorities are fostered, when the mentally or physically handicapped are assisted, when those on the margin of society are given a voice —in all these instances the dignity of life, and the sacredness of human life are furthered.... In particular, every contribution made to better the moral climate of society, to oppose permissiveness and hedonism, and all assistance to the family, which is the source of new life, effectively uphold the values of life" (May 26, 1978).

NEED FOR COURAGE

8. Much remains to be done to support those whose lives are wounded and to restore hope to those who are afraid of life. Courage is needed to resist pressures and false slogans, to proclaim the supreme

dignity of all life, and to demand that society itself give it its protection. A distinguished American, Thomas Jefferson, once stated: "The care of human life and happiness and not their destruction is the just and only legitimate object of good government" (March 31, 1809). I wish therefore to praise all the members of the Catholic Church and other Christian Churches, all men and women of the Judaeo-Christian heritage, as well as all people of good will who unite in common dedication for the defense of life in its fullness and for the promotion of all human rights.

Our celebration of life forms part of the celebration of the Eucharist. Our Lord and Savior, through His death and resurrection, has become for us "the bread of life" and the pledge of eternal life. In Him we find the courage, perseverance and inventiveness which we need in order to promote and defend life within our families and throughout the world.

Dear brothers and sisters: We are confident that Mary, the Mother of God and the Mother of life, will give us her help so that our way of living will always reflect our admiration and gratitude for God's gift of love that is life. We know that she will help us to use every day that is given to us as an opportunity to defend the life of the unborn and to render more human the lives of all our fellow human beings, wherever they may be.

And through the intercession of Our Lady of the Rosary, whose feast we celebrate today, may we come one day to the fullness of eternal life in Christ Jesus our Lord. Amen.

GOD BLESS AMERICA!

On Sunday evening, October 7, at Andrews Air Force Base, the Pope concluded his visit in the following address:

My dear friends in America, and my brothers and sisters in the faith of our Lord Jesus Christ,

As I leave this capital city of Washington, I wish to express my gratitude to the president of the United States and to all the religious and civil authorities of this country.

My thoughts turn likewise to all the American people: to all Catholics, Protestants and Jews, and to all men and women of good will, to people of every ethnic origin and in particular to the descendants of the first inhabitants of this land, the American Indians; to all of you whom I have greeted personally; those who have been close to me through the providential media of press, radio and television; those who have opened their hearts to me in so many ways. Your hospitality has been warm and filled with love, and I am grateful for all your kindnesses.

I believe strongly in the message of hope that I have held up to you, in the justice and love and truth that I have extolled, and in the peace that I have asked the Lord to give to all of you.

And now I must leave the United States and return to Rome. But all of you will constantly be remembered in my prayers, which I look upon as the best expression of my loyalty and friendship.

Today, therefore, my final prayer is this: that God may bless America, so that she may increasingly become—and truly be—and long remain—"One nation, *under God,* indivisible. With liberty and justice for all." God bless America! God bless America!

DEEP GRATITUDE, JOYFUL AND HEARTFELT

On his arrival at Fiumicino airport, Rome, at 8:30 a.m. on October 8, the Holy Father replied to the greeting of the Italian Prime Minister, Mr. Cossiga, as follows.

At the moment in which, after the unforgettable emotions of over a week of liturgical celebrations, meetings and talks, I set foot again on the soil of beloved Italy, a feeling of deep gratitude, joyful and heartfelt, rises from my spirit towards the Lord, who in His provident goodness has permitted me once more to talk personally with so many brothers and sons, and with such representative and authoritative men, men of good will.

The short days of my stay in Ireland enabled me to get to know that nation from close at hand, to admire its ancient traditions of faith, the testimonies of attachment to the Apostolic See, and to grasp its precious moral values. I am happy to have accepted the invitation of the Irish Bishops to celebrate with all those faithful the first centenary of the Marian apparition at Knock, to pay in this way a tribute of filial gratitude to Mary, who, in every country, offers evident and tangible signs of her motherly protection and her loving assistance, which we invoked mainly for peace and reconciliation in that beloved island.

My meeting, then, with the General Assembly of the United Nations, where the peoples of the world are represented and, so to speak, gathered, is in ideal continuity with the one that my unforgettable predecessor, Paul VI, carried out fourteen years ago, as part, and in the sign of, a persevering mission of peace. I, too, wished, in accepting with pleasure the invitation of the Secretary General of that Organization, to assure the nations that the Church is close to peacemakers and wishes to inspire and support their efforts, with the sole desire of rendering mankind a service. The Church wants, in fact, that peace which comes from the true conception of man, from respect for his rights and from the accomplishment of his duties, in a word, which is based on justice. She will never desist from calling on people to plan the future destinies of human society and of the world, with ever renewed and converted mentality.

Finally, meeting the desire of the President of the United States of America and of the most worthy members of that episcopate, I stayed for some days in the territory of their great country, on which an eminent task and a serious responsibility are incumbent—precisely because of the high level of prosperity and technico-social progress reached—with regard to the construction of a just world, worthy of man. It was first and foremost an ecclesial contact with the faithful and the pastors, in order to strengthen spirits and increase in them the courage to think and live "according to God and not according to men" (cf. Mk. 8:33).

The devoted and exultant welcome of the faithful and of the whole people of the United States has left in my heart the desire for a more and more direct and familiar contact with these beloved sons.

To conclude these brief remarks, I express in the first place to Mr. Prime Minister my deep and grateful satisfaction at the noble and fervent words with which he has welcomed me to Italian soil. With deep respect I also express due thanks to the Lords Cardinals, to the illustrious personalities of the Italian State and Government, to the distinguished members of the Diplomatic Corps, headed by their worthy Doyen, to the personalities of the Roman Curia, and finally to all those who wished to bid me this joyful welcome, making the hour of return more agreeable with their kind presence.

I then feel the pleasant duty of expressing my grateful satisfaction to the directors of the air companies, the pilots and crews of the aircraft, and all those who cooperated, with generous dedication, to the full success of this journey of mine.

While I present again to Christ the Lord, the Prince of Peace, the aspirations and resolutions of the peoples of the earth for serene coexistence, brotherly collaboration and human and Christian solidarity, I invoke with my apostolic blessing the divine outpourings of grace and mercy on you here present, on the beloved sons of Rome and of the whole of mankind.

A JOURNEY OF FAITH TO ANNOUNCE THE GOSPEL

At the beginning of the general audience on October 10 in St. Peter's Square, the Holy Father spoke about his journey to Ireland, the United Nations Organization and the United States, and announced that he would go on pilgrimage to the Sanctuary of Pompei on Sunday, October 21.

Beloved brothers and sisters in the Lord,

Here I am again back among you, after my pastoral journey to Ireland and to the United States!

After this event, such a joyful one for me, I feel again the need to thank warmly all those who contributed to its success. I thank those who welcomed me with such kindness, in the first place the President of Ireland, Mr. Hillery; the Secretary-General of the United Nations, Mr. Kurt Waldheim; the President of the United States, Mr. Carter; all the religious, civil and military authorities, and especially the episcopates. I thank those who transported me and accompanied me with such kind attention; I thank those who provided the service of order and security, and those who transmitted and commented on the various news reports of the various events. Above all, I thank with deep affection the immense crowds, which united round the Vicar of Christ in a brotherly and filial embrace, at every stage of my journey. But I want to thank you, too, who certainly prayed for me.

I always felt the spiritual closeness of millions and millions of persons who, with their prayer, made this journey of faith possible and certainly efficacious.

It was, in fact, solely a journey of faith, made solely to proclaim the Gospel, to "strengthen brothers," to console the afflicted, to bear witness to God's love, to point out to mankind its transcendent destiny.

Like St. Paul, I preached only Christ, and Christ crucified and risen again for us! (cf. 1 Cor. 1:23)

It was a journey of faith; therefore it was a journey of prayer, centered always on meditation of the Word of God, the celebration of the Eucharist and invocation of the Blessed Virgin.

It was also an "itinerant catechesis," in which it was my intention to stress everywhere, to all classes of persons, the true and ineffaceable patrimony of Catholic Doctrine.

It was also a journey of peace, love and brotherhood, which took me to the headquarters of the UNO. There above all, as in all the meetings with the crowds, in the name of Christ and of the Church, I became the spokesman of the peoples eager for justice and peace, on behalf of the poor, the suffering, the oppressed, the humble and children.

Together let us thank the Lord and Mary most holy for all this!

God grant that men may become better and better, more and more united and committed to good, forgiveness and brotherly love!

To thank the Blessed Virgin with all the greater fervor and implore the grace of conversion and peace, I announce to you now with immense joy that on Sunday, October 21, I will go on pilgrimage to the Sanctuary of Pompei.

I WENT ON PILGRIMAGE TO THE LIVING SHRINE OF THE PEOPLE OF GOD

The audience of Wednesday, October 17, was a particularly joyful one, with forty thousand people present in St. Peter's Square, bearing witness to the love with which the faithful of the whole world have followed the first year of John Paul II's pontificate and to their gratitude for all the Pope has done for the Church from the day of his election to the supreme ministry.

The Holy Father delivered the following address.

1. "The bishop who visits the communities of his Church is the true pilgrim who arrives every time at that particular shrine of the Good Pastor, which is the People of God, participating in Christ's royal priesthood. This shrine, in fact, is every man, whose 'mystery' can be explained and solved only in the mystery of the Word Incarnate *(Gaudium et spes,* no. 22)'' (cf. *Segno di contraddizione,* p. 160).

I was offered the opportunity to pronounce the above-mentioned words in the Matilda chapel, when Pope Paul VI invited me to preach the spiritual exercises in the Vatican.

These words come to my mind again today, since they seem to contain what was the most essential content of my journey to Ireland and to the United States, a journey occasioned by the invitation of the Secretary-General of UNO.

This journey, in both its stages, was actually a real *pilgrimage to the living shrine of the People of God.*

If the teaching of the Second Vatican Council permits us to look in this way at every visit of the Bishop to a parish, the same can be said also of that visit of the Pope. I think I have a special duty to express myself on this subject. It is also my deep wish that those who received me, with such hospitality, may know that I tried to become intimate with that mystery that Christ, the Good Shepherd, has molded and continues to mold in their souls, their history and their community. To highlight this, I have decided to interrupt, this Wednesday, the cycle of reflections on the words of Christ regarding the subject of marriage. We will resume it again in a week.

ON IRISH SOIL

2. I wish in the first place to bear witness to the meeting with the mystery of the Church *in the land of Ireland.* I will never forget that place, in which we stopped for a short time, in the early morning hours, on Sunday, September 30: *Clonmacnois.* The ruins of the abbey and of the church speak of the life that once pulsated there. It is a question of one of those monasteries in which Irish monks not only implanted Christianity in the Emerald Isle, but also took it from there to the other countries of Europe. It is difficult to look at those ruins merely as a monument of the past; whole generations of Europe owe to them the light of the Gospel and the structural framework of their culture. Those ruins are still charged with a great mission. They still constitute a challenge. They still speak of that fullness of life to which Christ has called us. It is difficult for a pilgrim to arrive at those places without those traces of the apparently dead past revealing to him a permanent and everlasting dimen-

sion of life. Here is Ireland: at the heart of the perennial mission of the Church, which St. Patrick started.

Following as a pilgrim in his footsteps, we move in the direction of the primatial See of Armagh, and we stop, on the way, at Drogheda, where, for the occasion, the relics of St. Oliver Plunkett, Bishop and Martyr, were solemnly displayed. Only by kneeling in front of those relics can one express the whole truth about historical and contemporary Ireland and also touch its wounds, confident that they will heal and not prevent the whole organism from pulsating with the fullness of life.

We also touch, therefore, the painful problems of today, but we do not cease our pilgrimage through that magnificent shrine of the People of God, which opens up before us, in so many places, in so many marvelous liturgical assemblies, during the celebrations of the Eucharist at Dublin, Galway, Knock (the Marian Sanctuary), Maynooth and Limerick. In particular I have and always will have present in my thought also the meeting with the President of Ireland, Mr. Patrick J. Hillery, and with the illustrious authorities of that nation. Let all those I met—the priests, missionaries, religious men and women, pupils, laity, married couples and parents, Irish youth, the sick—and above all my beloved brothers in the episcopate—let them all remember that I was present in their midst as a pilgrim, visiting the Shrine of the Good Shepherd, who dwells in the whole People of God; that I walked through that magnificent river bed of the history of salvation, which from the times of St. Patrick has become the Emerald Isle, with head bent and grateful heart, seeking together with them. the ways that lead to the future.

ACROSS THE OCEAN TO THE U.S.A.

3. I wish to say the same thing also to my brothers and sisters beyond the ocean. Their Church is still young, because their great society is young: there have passed only two centuries of its history on the political map of the globe. I wish to thank them all, for the welcome they gave me; for their response to this visit, this presence, necessarily a short one. I confess that I was surprised by this welcome and this response. We persisted in pouring rain during the Mass for the young, the first evening, at Boston. The rain accompanied us along the streets of that city, as also along the streets of New York, among the skyscrapers. That rain did not prevent so many men of good will from persevering in prayer, from waiting for the moment of my arrival, for my word and my blessing.

Unforgettable for me are the districts of Harlem, with its Negro population in the majority; South Bronx, with the newcomers from Latin-American countries; the meeting with the young in Madison Square Garden and in Battery Park in torrential rain and a raging storm, and in the stadium at Brooklyn, when the sun finally appeared. And the preceding day the vast Yankee Stadium, packed full for participation in the Eucharistic liturgy. And then: illustrious Philadelphia, the first capital of the independent States with its bell of freedom, and perhaps nearly two million participants in the afternoon Mass, in the very center of the city. And the meeting with rural America at Des Moines. Afterwards Chicago, in which it was possible, in a more appropriate way, to develop the analogy on the subject "e pluribus unum." Finally, the city of Washington, the capital of the United States, with all its heavy program, up to the last Mass with the Capitol in the background.

The Bishop of Rome, in the steps of the Good Shepherd, entered as a pilgrim His sanctuary in the new continent and tried to live, together with you, the reality of the Church, which emerges from the teaching of the Second Vatican Council, with all the depth and rigor this doctrine brings with it. It seems, in fact, that all that was accompanied above all by great joy, at the fact that we are this Church; that we are the people to whom the Father offers redemption and salvation in His Son and in the Holy Spirit. Joy at the fact that— among all the tensions of modern civilization, of the economy and politics—there exists precisely this dimension of human life on the earth; and that we participate in it. Although our attention is directed also to these tensions, which we wish to solve in a human and worthy way, the divine joy of the People, which becomes aware that it is the People of God, and that as such it seeks its own unity, is, however, greater and full of hope.

AT THE UNITED NATIONS

4. In this context, also the words spoken before the United Nations Organization became a particular fruit of my pilgrimage over these important stages of the history of the whole Church and of Christianity. What else could I say before that supreme "Forum" of a political character, but what constitutes the very core of the Gospel message? The words of a great love for man, which lives in the communities of so many peoples and nations, within the frontiers of so many

states and political systems. If political activity, in the dimensions of the single states and in international dimensions, must ensure a real primacy of man on earth, if it must serve his real dignity, the witness of the spirit and of truth borne by Christianity and the Church, is necessary. And therefore, on behalf of Christianity and the Church, I am grateful to all those who wished to listen to my words at UNO, New York, on October 2, 1979.

In the same way I am deeply grateful for the welcome that the President of the United States, Mr. Jimmy Carter, gave me on October 6, at the historic meeting in the White House with him and his dear family, and with all the high authorities gathered there.

5. "We are unworthy servants; we have only done what was our duty" (Lk. 17:10). This is what Christ taught His apostles. I, too, with these words that spring from my deepest conviction, conclude my allocution today, the necessity of which was dictated by the importance of my recent journey. Let me repay, at least in this way, the great debt I have contracted to the Good Shepherd and to those who opened up the ways of my peregrination.

INDEX

Daughters of St. Paul

IN MASSACHUSETTS
    50 St. Paul's Ave. Jamaica Plain, Boston, Ma. 02130
    172 Tremont Street, Boston, Ma. 02111
IN NEW YORK
    78 Fort Place, Staten Island, N.Y. 10301
    59 East 43rd Street, New York, N.Y. 10017
    7 State Street (at Mother Seton Shrine), New York, N.Y. 10004
    625 East 187th Street, Bronx, N.Y. 10458
    525 Main Street, Buffalo, N.Y. 14203
IN NEW JERSEY
    Hudson Mall — Route 440 and
      Communipaw Avenue, Jersey City, N.J. 07304
IN CONNECTICUT
    202 Fairfield Avenue, Bridgeport, Ct. 06604
IN OHIO
    2105 Ontario St. (at Prospect Ave.), Cleveland, Oh. 44115
    25 E. Eighth Street, Cincinnati, Oh. 45202
IN PENNSYLVANIA
    1719 Chestnut Street, Philadelphia, Pa. 19103
IN FLORIDA
    2700 Biscayne Blvd., Miami, Fl. 33137
IN LOUISIANA
    4403 Veterans Memorial Blvd., Metairie, La. 70002
    1800 South Acadian Thruway, P.O. Box 2028, Baton Rouge, La. 70821
IN MISSOURI
    1001 Pine Street (at North 10th), St. Louis, Mo. 63101
IN ILLINOIS
    172 North Michigan Avenue, Chicago, Ill. 60601
IN TEXAS
    114 Main Plaza, San Antonio, Tx. 78205
IN CALIFORNIA
    1570 Fifth Avenue, San Diego, Ca. 92101
    46 Geary Street, San Francisco, Ca. 94108
IN HAWAII
    1143 Bishop Street, Honolulu, Hi. 96813
IN ALASKA
    750 West 5th Avenue, Anchorage, Ak. 99501
IN CANADA
    3022 Dufferin Street, Toronto 395, Ontario, Canada
IN ENGLAND
    57, Kensington Church Street, London W. 8, England
IN AUSTRALIA
    58 Abbotsford Rd., Homebush, N.S.W., Sydney 2140, Australia